Dedication

Oscar Gordon, you've been with me through thick and thin – from high school drama plays, to cleaning toilets to pay for flights for an audition in LA, to filming me dumpster-diving for food in New York with zero budget. There have been so many adventures and I look forward to many more. I cannot thank you enough for being a real mate – one who is always honest and can tell it to me straight. You inspire me to be my best. And let's be honest … you're pretty funny. You can always put a smile on my face. I feel very lucky to have you in my life, Oscar – you're a real soul with a great heart and you are so special to me.

LOLA BERRY

THE HAPPY LIFE

Pan Macmillan Australia

plum.

Introduction 6
Essential ingredients 8

Nourishment 13
Happy eating 16
Coming off sugar 16
Water 18
Looking like a model 22
A little word on calories 22
Ethical food 22
Planning meals 24
Mindful eating 24
My day on a plate 25

Mind 53
Emotional eating 56
Confidence 59
Resilience 62
Values 64
Gratitude 66

Body 113
Exercise 116
Yoga 118
Sleep 130
Detoxing your life 132
Crystal power 140

CONTENTS

Recipes
Brekkie 27
Savoury stuff 69
Sweet stuff 143
Drinks 197

Soul 179
Meditation 182
Mindfulness 185
Nature 186
Gardening 190
Kindness 192
Being with animals 195

Friendship 231
Being a good friend 234

Intimacy 237
Vulnerability 240
Being yourself from the get-go 242
Dealing with conflict 244
Break-ups 246

Career 249
Opportunity 253
How to make a dream book 254

Travel 259
Food 262
Sleep 264
Exercise 264
Soul 265

Thanks 266
Index 268

Introduction

Happiness. It's the big one. It's what we all want. Many of us believe we'll be happy when we get that dream job, or buy that car/house/stuff, or go on that holiday, or get that great body. For me, happiness is not something we 'get' from having stuff or status — it's a kind of peaceful feeling that everything is part of a bigger picture and I don't need to know all the answers. It's about being in the moment, loving what I'm doing, loving who I am and who I'm sharing time with — everything is in flow and I'm part of that flow. To me that's living the dream.

Researchers like Sonja Lyubomirsky and Martin Seligman have been studying happiness for yonks and yonks, and they've found that it's got very little to do with our life circumstances (career, social status, possessions or stuff that happens to us) and way more to do with how we respond to those circumstances (our thoughts, intentions and actions). Lyubomirsky says that genetics accounts for 50 per cent of our happiness 'set point', circumstances 10 per cent and the other 40 per cent comes from intentional activity, such as being kind, caring and giving to other people, taking care of our health and practising spirituality. I love these stats because it shows that we have much more of a say in our happiness than we might think, which is awesome news!

The truth is, you have everything you need to be happy right here, right now — it's all up to you. I know that sounds kind of scary, but it's also really empowering. It means you're in charge; you're not waiting for someone else or something else to get the ball rolling.

The first step? Trust yourself. You know loads more than you give yourself credit for. I've heard people say that our intuition is spot-on 90 per cent of the time, but I believe it's more like 99 per cent of the time. When something feels right we just find ourselves doing it; time stops and for that moment nothing else matters. We've tapped into our deepest intelligence. I call this 'thinking with our hearts'. On the flip side, we also know when something feels wrong, when our heart's not in it. The trick is being able to act on that innate intelligence, without letting negative thoughts talk us out of it.

Clients often tell me they've known for a long time that they want to make big lifestyle changes, but that they 'don't have the time', their family/partner 'won't eat healthy food', they need to 'wait until after a birthday (or Christmas or whatever)', they 'just don't have the willpower' or they 'refuse to be seen in public in a tracksuit/leotard/bathers' ... on and on the excuses go.

Trust me, I've been there. I was the queen of excuses: 'I'm too busy', 'I'm travelling' and 'I don't want to appear rude by refusing their food'. It took me a while, but I now understand that all of these excuses were a reflection of my lack of self-respect. I had to learn to put myself first, to stop judging myself and worrying about what other people thought of me, to see myself as a kind and loving person. This book is a collection of all of the ways I have learned to do just that, including eating real food that nourishes my body and mind and makes me feel awesome; getting lots of sleep; being out in nature; doing my walks and yoga; being kind to people; and practising mindfulness.

Throughout the book, I've included deliciously healthy recipes that will have you feeling great and glowing from the inside out. There are also tips on getting a good night's sleep, becoming more mindful and creating a dream book, plus I talk about the importance of failure, of random acts of kindness and of the healing power of nature and animals. For me, this book is all heart; it's real, open and honest and I'll be rapt if it helps you on your journey to self-love. Because when you truly love who you are, the most *amazing* shift happens. You notice that you stop judging people, that you can roll with the flow, that you trust the process of life, knowing that everything happens for a reason. You have this glow about you and people want to know more, they're intrigued by your energy. So people come into your life and opportunities arise. But enough talk — let's get started. It's time to get in touch with your awesomeness!

Lola xx

essential INGREDIENTS

Notes on the recipes

* Cooking temperatures are for a regular or conventional oven. If you are using a fan-forced oven, you'll need to drop the cooking temperature by 10–20°C (check your oven manual).
* Wherever possible, all the foods I eat and use in my recipes are whole, raw, organic, seasonal, unprocessed and as close to their natural state as possible. If you can, do the same.

Almond butter

This ground almond paste, with all its lovely oils, is a wonderful butter substitute. I prefer mine raw (not roasted) because it's the healthier option. Almonds are loaded with fibre, good fats and protein, plus they've got a fair bit of magnesium and calcium.

Almond meal (almond flour)

This grain-free flour is another kitchen staple. Whole almond meal has a coarse texture and is great in brekkie creations, for crumbing meats and fish, and even in desserts and raw treats. Blanched almond meal (often called almond flour) is more refined, as the almond skin is removed before grinding.

Almond milk

You can add unsweetened almond milk to pretty much any recipe that calls for milk. You can make your own almond milk if you have a powerful food processor. (Don't throw away the nutty, fibrous bits: use them to make energy balls or other raw treats.)

Amaranth

I use this Aztec seed like a grain. It's great combined with quinoa, millet and buckwheat groats to make a paleo granola. This is more birdseedy than regular sugary granolas, but it acts like an intestinal broom and is full of fibre, minerals and vitamins.

Avocado oil

This is so good for you. It has a deep-green colour and creamy flavour, and is best used for salad dressings and adding at the end of a meal rather than in cooking (it goes rancid if heated too high).

Avocados

Avocados are a good source of fibre, potassium and vitamin C, and although they are high in fat, it's the good kind (unsaturated, like olive oil). My favourite variety is Hass, which is available all year round.

Bee pollen

Bee pollen is the soft yellow 'dust' from flowers that bees brush into the pollen sacs on their back legs. Bees use it to feed their larvae and to make royal jelly, and it's high in protein and nutrients. People with pollen allergies should avoid bee pollen; vegans might prefer to leave it out, too. I sprinkle it on pancakes, muesli or even porridge, and it makes a great smoothie topper.

Black beans

Also called black turtle beans, these are related to kidney beans and haricot (navy) beans and are widely used in American, Creole, Cajun and South American dishes. They are high in protein and fibre, so a great vegetarian option. Don't confuse them with black beans (*douchi*) used in Asian cuisines, which are fermented and salted soybeans. (I don't use soy products in my recipes because my body can't tolerate them and because most soy grown is genetically modified.)

Black peppercorns

I reckon freshly ground black peppercorns taste loads better than the pre-ground stuff. If a recipe calls for a more subtle taste of black pepper, I just grind it more with my mortar and pestle.

Buckwheat

Despite its name, buckwheat is not a grain but the fruit of a plant related to sorrel and rhubarb. It's sold as groats or flour. Groats are the light-coloured kernels that you can buy whole or ground (cracked) and either raw or roasted (called

ESSENTIAL INGREDIENTS

kasha). Buckwheat flour is available in light and dark versions. The darker type contains more of the hull, therefore more fibre and nutrients, and has a stronger, nuttier flavour. I love to use buckwheat groats for porridge or as a replacement for burghul (cracked wheat) in tabouli. Buckwheat flour makes delicious pancakes and slices, and I often add it to gluten-free recipes.

Cacao

Technically, cacao and cocoa are the same thing, but in everyday use, cacao usually refers to the raw, unprocessed beans, and cocoa to the beans that are roasted and processed (and usually combined with milk and sugar to make chocolate). Raw cacao powder is the healthiest way to get a chocolate hit; add it to a smoothie, or make a hot chocolate, energy balls or a raw choccy cake. It's delicious and full of health benefits, especially for our brains. It's high in magnesium (great for our muscles and heart) and phenylalanine, a precursor to two brain chemicals that make us feel good (norepinephrine and dopamine) – maybe that's why we love chocolate so much!

Chia seeds

Chia seeds provide an amazing hit of nutrients, especially protein, calcium and omega-3 fatty acids. To get the full benefits, soak the seeds – even five minutes is enough. They're quite gelatinous, so people use them to thicken sauces and as a substitute for eggs. I add them to my brekkie every day, and sprinkle them on smoothies and salads. Don't boil or bake them at high temperatures as it reduces their nutrients.

Chilli

Chillies speed up your metabolic rate (good for weight control), promote heart health, and are full of antioxidants (great for your skin). I slice them up fresh to have in salads or veggie dishes or to season meat, and sometimes I even add a tiny pinch of flakes to smoothies, slices and cakes. The mildest chilli is the longish, thin cayenne chilli (it comes in red, green and yellow), followed by the medium–hot ball chilli, the hot jalapeño, the very hot, tiny bird's eye chilli and the scorching habañero. I have used the milder cayenne chillies for most of the recipes in this book.

Coconut, dried

You can get desiccated, that's super-fine; shredded, which is long, thin pieces; or flaked, which is chunky and chewy. I love them all, and you'll find them throughout my recipes.

Coconut flour

Coconut flour is quite dense and needs help sticking together, so if I'm making coconut-flour pancakes, for example, I will add an extra egg to help the mixture bind. But it tastes brill!

Coconut milk and coconut cream

These are great for curries, pancake mixes, porridge and smoothies. Coconut milk and cream are made the same way, just using different amounts of water. You can make them yourself or buy them ready-made. If possible, buy organic coconut milk and cream packed in BPA-free tins (BPA is a toxic chemical that works like oestrogen and can affect your hormones).

Coconut oil

Coconut oil is solid at cooler temperatures. Unlike regular olive oil (not extra-virgin), coconut oil doesn't break down or go rancid when cooked at high temperatures – making it a winner. People worry about coconut oil making them fat. It is a saturated fat, but it's a medium-chain fatty acid, which means the body can use it quickly (rather than having to store it). It's awesome used topically, too – I use it to moisturise my face and body. It's also thermogenic, meaning it helps to speed up your metabolism.

Coconut syrup

This has a slightly stronger flavour than honey or even agave – almost like a mild molasses. It's loaded with minerals and contains less fructose than agave and honey, too. But remember, it's still a sweetener, so use it in moderation.

Coconut water

Coconut water is the liquid from young coconuts – a bit like Mother Nature's very own electrolyte drink. It's naturally sweet. It makes a fantastic base for smoothies and, if you're a cocktail fan, then it's great mixed with your favourite alcohol (and the electrolytes will help to prevent a hangover!).

Dates, medjool

Dates are a great source of the electrolyte potassium, which is a key player for heart health. Plus, they're full of fibre and will keep you regular. Medjool dates are bigger, sweeter and squidgier than regular dried dates. They're very sweet, though, so to avoid a sugar rush when snacking on them I pop the seed out and replace it with a Brazil nut. The protein and fat from the nut help to lower the glycaemic load and make for a slower release of energy.

ESSENTIAL INGREDIENTS

Eggs
I always choose organic and free-range eggs, because they taste unreal and because the chickens have access to pasture, sunlight and a much better life than caged hens.

Goji berries
These berries are a great source of antioxidants and have a nice flavour – not too sweet, a bit like a sourish sultana. You can add them to any dish (sweet or savoury): sprinkle them on your brekkie or your salads, use them in a raw nut mix, or even in your tea.

Herbs and spices
Fresh herbs and spices are the key to adding flavour to your food creations, not to mention the antioxidant hit you'll reap from them. Some of my favourites are cinnamon, nutmeg, paprika, chilli flakes, cumin, coriander seeds, cardamom, fennel, dill, rosemary . . . wow, the list goes on!

Honey, raw
Raw honey has been filtered, but in a way that doesn't destroy its nutrients. It is not pasteurised (the heating and filtration process that makes it clear), so all its beneficial enzymes are still present. Raw honey can be solid at room temperature (depending on how cold it is), and is milky (not clear). It's about twice as sweet as sugar, so you don't need to use as much.

Linseed (flaxseed)
Linseed (also called flaxseed) is a great source of fibre, and high in omega-3 fatty acids and minerals. I always tell my vegan clients to up the flaxseeds and flaxseed oil. You can get brown flax and golden flax, but both contain the same nutrients. To really release the nutrients, the seeds need to be ground up. I never bake or cook with linseed as heat destroys its nutrients.

LSA
LSA stands for (ground) linseed, sunflower seeds and almond, and is an awesome superfood. It's high in fibre, good fats and veggo protein, plus it has a nice hit of B vitamins. I use it in smoothies, raw creations and breakfast combos and on top of salads. I don't cook or bake with LSA as the flax and sunflower seeds lose their nutritional benefits when heated.

Macadamia nuts and oil
Macadamia nuts are an excellent source of mono-unsaturated fats and a top brain food. I love their texture and flavour and use them in brekkies, smoothies, salads and baking. Macadamia oil is so pure I even use it on my skin.

Maple syrup
Maple syrup is a wonderful sweetener: it has a great flavour, is full of minerals and has less fructose than honey, dates or agave. Make sure you choose 100 per cent syrup, not the imitation stuff. It costs more, but it's much healthier.

Millet
This is an ancient seed that we use like a grain. It's gluten-free so great for any paleo creation. Rinse millet before using. I love to add a little to a mash to give it more depth, use it to make a creamy coconut porridge, and just cook it up the same way I would rice or quinoa.

Nut milks
You can whip up your own nut milks easily: all you need is a handful of raw nuts (always use raw for nut milks), a couple of cups of water and a good blender – then whiz it up. Sometimes I add nutmeg and cinnamon so it's like a nut-milk chai. And you can either keep the pulp in (it's full of fibre) or strain it with a nut-milk bag or muslin cloth, then use that pulp to make a raw treat the next day.

Nuts and seeds
Nuts and seeds are a brilliant source of good fats. When my recipes say to soak and rinse nuts, this means soak them in water for 2–3 hours (or overnight if possible) then rinse. This removes enzyme inhibitors and makes them easier to digest. After rinsing (unless you're about to blend them up for a smoothie or raw treat), spread the nuts out on a baking tray and place in a 50°C oven or dehydrator to dry out (this will take anywhere from 6–24 hours depending on the temperature). Store your activated nuts in sealed glass jars in the pantry.

Oats
Pure oats don't contain gluten, but because of the way we process them, most oatmeal brands have been cross-contaminated with minuscule amounts of wheat, barley and/or rye, so we can't call them 'gluten-free'. About 30 per cent of people who have coeliac disease cannot tolerate oats (even when the cross-contamination is almost eliminated), so if you have coeliac disease, or a particularly severe gluten allergy, proceed with caution.

Olive oil, extra-virgin
Olive oil is a great source of mono-unsaturated fat. Regular olive oil becomes unstable and rancid

when used in cooking at high temperatures, but I've been jazzed to discover recently that good-quality extra-virgin varieties are much higher in polyphenols (that's the antioxidant part of the olive oil) and this prevents the double bond in the mono-unsaturated fat from breaking. Just make sure the oil you buy is extra-virgin, which means it's been pressed once, with no chemicals or additives. And good quality, of course, if you're going to cook with it.

Pomegranate

Pomegranate seeds are packed with antioxidants. I have them fresh in salads. Dried seeds are also great in salads and trail mixes and as smoothie toppers. The juice is great, but make sure you get the 100 per cent pure juice.

Pumpkin seeds

Also known as pepitas, pumpkin seeds are full of zinc, an important mineral for health. Zinc is found in every cell of our body and plays a big role in immunity, cell division, cell growth, wound healing and the breakdown of carbs.

Quinoa

This seed is packed with nutrients and is very high in protein, so it's excellent if you're a veggo or vegan. It's also versatile: you can get quinoa seeds, quinoa flakes, puffed quinoa, and even quinoa milk and quinoa flour. There is white quinoa, red and a royal black, though they're pretty much on a par nutrient-wise (the coloured ones may have a slightly higher mineral content). I find the white has the mildest flavour. You cook it in a similar way to rice and it suits both sweet and savoury dishes. You can use the flakes to make a porridge for brekkie, the seeds as the base of a superfood salad for lunch or with curry for dinner, and the flour for making cakes, muffins and pancakes.

Salt

I love to use pink salt in my cooking. It tastes just like normal salt but has loads more minerals (about 84 trace minerals, in fact). It's great to use in place of regular table salt and looks pretty. I use Murray River or Himalayan. Celtic salt and rock salt are healthy options, too. Use salt sparingly, though, and stay away from the bleached stuff.

Stevia

Stevia, which is made from the leaves of a South American herb, is about 300 times sweeter than sugar and has no calories and no impact on blood sugar levels. You can buy it in powder form or as a liquid. Use it sparingly – if you use more than a couple of drops of liquid you'll get a pretty nasty aftertaste. It doesn't taste quite the same as sugar, but once you're used to it, you'll be converted.

Sugar

Some of the sugars used in the recipes in this book are: coconut nectar and coconut sugar – both derived from the sap of coconut-palm flowers; rapadura/panela – unrefined whole cane sugar, made from dehydrated cane juice; and moscavo – unrefined cane sugar. When it comes to sugars, even the natural ones, remember they are sweeteners so use them sparingly, as treats.

Tahini

Tahini is a paste made from crushed sesame seeds. You can buy hulled (where the seed casing has been removed) and unhulled (made from the whole seed). Both are high in protein and good fats. Hulled tahini is lighter in colour and has a milder taste; unhulled has more calcium and fibre. You can also get black tahini, which tastes similar to hulled tahini. Tahini is great in salad dressings, dips and energy balls.

Tea

I love herbal teas, as they're an ace way to add a whole lot of nutritional value to your diet. They can be as simple as adding a knob of ginger to a cup of hot water or as intriguing as blossoming flowers. I love Brahmi (an ancient Indian herb used in Ayurvedic medicine) for brain power, lavender for calming the nervous system, chamomile for digestion and thyme for the immune system.

Vanilla pods

Vanilla-bean pods, like honey and cinnamon, are a great libido enhancer. Wrap the pods in foil, seal them in a zip-lock bag, and store them in a cool, dark place so they don't dry out. Vanilla pods can be pricey, but you can always use powdered vanilla (make sure it's 100 per cent vanilla) or vanilla extract (not chemically produced essence) instead.

Yoghurt

Some people who react badly to cow's milk can tolerate yoghurt as it's partially fermented and is a little easier to digest. Choose organic or biodynamic full-cream options as they're more nutritious than low-fat yoghurt. If you can't handle cow's milk yoghurt, try sheep's or goat's milk yoghurt – they have a slightly stronger flavour. Then there are coconut or nut milk yoghurts for a vegan option. Always read the label carefully: you don't want any added sugar or gelatine. We're after real foods, as close to their natural state as possible.

Choosing which foods to eat can get really confusing — even for me and I'm a nutritionist! I mean, there is always so much new research on the physiological effects of different nutrients, not to mention all the different sustainability and ethical considerations. For me, though, the bottom line has always been to keep things simple and choose 'real' food. By real food I mean minimally processed ingredients that are as close to their natural state as possible. Think fresh fruit and veggies, nuts and seeds, and ethically produced sources of protein like meat, chicken, fish and eggs.

All of the recipes in this book (like those in my 20/20 Diet books) are inspired by the paleo principle that our bodies thrive best on the foods that our hunter-gatherer ancestors ate. However, unlike hardcore paleo followers, I do like to use buckwheat, quinoa, millet and oats because they offer brilliant health benefits. Quinoa, for example, is very high in protein (awesome for vegetarians) and buckwheat is a great source of the bioflavonoid rutin, which has antioxidant properties. I'm also a big fan of fermented foods because they build healthy gut flora, which in turn strengthens the immune system and enhances overall health. And unlike most paleos, I'm not averse to partially fermented dairy products like yoghurt and goat's cheese, and the occasional knob of butter.

HAPPY eating

Happy eating starts with listening to your body. If you feel tired and bloated after you eat pasta or bread, it might be a sign that you need to try ditching wheat for a while. Or if you feel a bit nauseous or gassy after drinking milk, you might need to go easy on the dairy. Even refined sugars can make some people feel very upset in the tummy, while for others, soy milk causes diarrhoea. It's really about tuning in to your body.

However, paying attention to what your body is telling you is only the first step – you've also got to be prepared to act on the messages it's giving you. This is the tricky part – choosing to nourish yourself with real food because you genuinely care about your health, because you value yourself and believe that you're worth it. It's harder to take care of your health if deep down you don't respect who you are. I talk more about this later in the book.

Happy eating is not about rigid rules, crazy detoxes and obsessing about the foods you can't eat. It's about focusing on all the amazing foods you can have in abundance and how awesome you'll feel when you eat them. And if you do have a favourite treat then I'm a big believer in finding a healthy alternative. Happy eating is not about missing out – it's about falling back in love with real foods and enjoying every moment of their preparation and every mouthful of their goodness.

Coming off sugar

One of the first questions I ask my clients is 'What foods do you crave?' The most common answer is chocolate, followed by ice cream, though quite a few people also crave cheese, fries or potato crisps. Some food cravings can be linked to mineral deficiencies and others to lack of protein; even a bad night's sleep will affect the kind of foods you're craving. However, these cravings will generally go away once the cause is addressed.

An addiction, however, is different. The body experiences unpleasant physiological changes ('withdrawal') when a particular substance is not available – think the headaches and fogginess people get when they miss their morning coffee. Sugar, however, is far worse, and many studies show that it's more addictive than hardcore drugs.

So how does it work? Well, when we eat something sweet, it activates the reward centre in our brain so we feel buzzed and happy. (We're actually wired to seek out sweet foods because our brains need a constant supply of glucose to keep functioning. Even looking at something sweet can jack up our dopamine levels!) However, to keep everything in balance, the pancreas secretes insulin to mop up any excess glucose and store it as glycogen in the liver and muscles. (Too much glucose is actually toxic to the body; that's why people with diabetes are at risk of developing heart disease, blindness, nerve and organ damage, and other serious conditions.) When the insulin has done its job, the sudden drop in blood glucose is the 'crash' we feel after a sugar binge (tiredness, low mood), so we reach for the sugar again, creating the binge cycle that leads us to weight gain and puts us at risk of developing obesity, insulin resistance, diabetes and all the other health problems we're seeing in epidemic proportions.

Does that mean we can't have any sugar? Not at all. We just need to have way less of it. Australians are currently downing about 30–40 teaspoons of sugar per day in coffee, tea, soft drinks, fruit juices, cereals, breads, bikkies, sauces and processed foods. The World Health Organization now recommends that added

sugar (including fruit juice and dried fruit but excluding the natural sugar in fruit, veggies and milk products) should comprise no more than 10 per cent of our daily energy intake (about 9–10 teaspoons for the 'average' adult). It also says that if we could knock our added sugar down to 5 per cent (roughly 5–6 teaspoons a day), we'd get even greater health benefits.

I don't use refined table sugar in any of my recipes (except in kombucha, but that doesn't count because the good bacteria eat it all up in the fermentation process). To sweeten breakfasts, desserts and energy snacks, I prefer instead to use honey, maple syrup or coconut sugar. I don't use stacks of these either (somewhere between ½ teaspoon and 2 teaspoons per serve for most recipes), or I use stevia drops (300 times sweeter than sugar). If you want to use even less sugar, go for it, though steer clear of artificial sweeteners like saccharin, aspartame and sucralose because they can still mess with your dopamine pathways and cause digestive problems such as bloating and diarrhoea.

If you're used to eating a lot of sugar, be aware that the first week you cut down is always the hardest, so go easy on yourself. Have plenty of nuts or energy balls at the ready to snack on whenever you feel cravings. Your body will respond to real food fast: you'll notice that you start to feel better within 48 hours of ditching all that junk. After a couple of weeks, you'll notice your tastebuds change, too, so that even a carrot stick or a wedge of baked pumpkin tastes like the most delicious treat ever!

And enjoy the new habits you are creating for yourself. It takes time for our brains to form new pathways and for the old ones to weaken, so you may as well enjoy the ride. Don't be afraid to be 'that' person who asks if there is any sugar in the sauce or if they can have their dressing on the side. This is about your health and wellbeing. Put yourself first, not what you imagine others might think of you. And don't apologise. Be honest and firm but not preachy or rude. Then people will learn to respect you and your health choices; after all, they're your choices.

Water

Water is critically important for the healthy functioning of the human body. If we don't have enough of it, our skin dries, it can become much harder to focus and we might not be as regular on the loo, to name just a few signs of poor hydration. Did you know that the first sign of dehydration is hunger? So next time you're reaching for a snack, try a glass of water first. It will keep you hydrated and help you stick to healthy eating habits. Interestingly, headaches at the front of the head can be caused by dehydration, so next time you have a frontal headache, try the glass-of-water trick!

How much do I need?

We need about 1 litre of water per 22 kilograms of body weight per day. I know that sounds like a lot but the trick is to slowly increase it. Don't go from one glass to 3 litres – you'll be running to the loo all day. Just slowly increase your water intake. Another trick is to keep your water bottle on your desk to remind you to drink. I love using a glass, swing-top bottle (or a clear BPA-free plastic one), so I can see how much I'm drinking, but a good-quality stainless steel or aluminium container is just as good – getting the fluid into your body is the important thing!

What if I don't like the taste?

Many clients tell me that they can't bear the thought of having to drink so much water because they find the taste so boring. This is usually at the start of our work together, so I know that once their tastebuds start shifting, they will come to really enjoy pure, clean water. In the meantime, if this is you, get creative with your water by adding mint leaves, berries, or thin slices of lemon, orange and/or lime. (Don't squeeze in any citrus juice as it can erode tooth enamel if you're sipping on it all day.) Even cucumber slices taste great in a bottle of water.

Healing water

I know this sounds a bit hippie, but try writing positive affirmations on your water bottle. I always have words like 'love', 'dream', 'passion', 'courage' and 'brave' written on mine. I get a little warm feeling every time I take a swig of water, plus it's a great conversation starter. Sometimes I even put water-based crystals like rose quartz or amethyst in my water bottle as well, which look beautiful and make me feel like I am drinking in love and beauty. But if you want to try this, please be very careful. Not all crystals can be used this way as they may contain heavy metals that can make you quite sick. So when you buy your crystals explain that you are using them for your water bottle and that you need water-based ones.

Looking like a model

I'd be lying if I said I didn't want to look like a Victoria's Secret model, but I'm well aware that this is a totally unrealistic goal – for starters, I'm 5 foot 3 inches (160 cm) tall! I've also learned that beauty has less to do with your appearance and more to do with your attitude and mindset. We are all built differently, so comparing yourself to others is a waste of time. The best thing you can do is to focus on being the very best version of you. And the easiest place to begin? Nourishment, sleep and exercise. I tell you, it's that healthy glow that turns people's heads – that's what makes people really notice you; that's what's attractive. Aim for the glow! Or, even easier, just smile. You will be at your most beautiful.

A little word on calories

I don't recommend counting calories/kilojoules if you are trying to change your eating habits, as it takes all the joy and fun out of food. Of course some foods are denser than others, but at the end of the day if you're eating an abundance of veggies, fresh fruit, raw nuts and seeds and ethically sourced protein, you won't need to count calories. Think real food and real nourishment and watch the body respond – it wants to thrive.

Another reason to give calorie-counting a miss is that not all calories have the same effects in the body. Protein, for example, takes a lot more energy (25–30 per cent) to digest, absorb and metabolise than carbs (6–8 per cent) or fat (2–3 per cent). Plus, it makes us feel full, which reduces our appetite.

Also, the two simplest forms of sugar, glucose and fructose, have completely different effects in the body. Fructose, way more than glucose, stimulates our hunger hormone ghrelin, while at the same time reducing our satiety hormone leptin, meaning we can eat loads more of it. Ordinary table sugar (sucrose) is actually made up of fructose and glucose, and while every cell in our bodies can metabolise glucose, fructose can only be metabolised in significant amounts in the liver. This means any excess is stored as triglycerides (fats) in the liver, which researchers believe at least partly explains the rise in obesity, heart disease, fatty liver disease (insulin resistance) and diabetes (what some people are calling 'diabesity').

The 'fat is bad' myth

For decades (it started in the late 1960s) we were told that eating fat was bad for our health. Everything was labelled 'low fat', and to compensate for the loss in texture and flavour a stack of sugar was added, though it was hidden under labels such as maltose, dextrose and high-fructose corn syrup. It wasn't until researchers began to notice a sharp increase in heart disease and diabetes, despite our consuming far less fat in our diets, that the myth was dispelled. For me, it doesn't make sense to restrict our intake of fats. The body needs fats to thrive. Triglycerides, cholesterol and other essential fatty acids (fats the body can't make on its own) store energy, insulate us and protect our vital organs. They also act as messengers in the body, initiating chemical reactions that help control growth, immune function, reproduction and other aspects of basic metabolism. Every cell membrane contains lipids (fats). Plus, our brain cells (neurons) have a protective coating on their axons called myelin that speeds up the transmission of electrical impulses in our brains. Why would we deprive our body of a nutrient vital to its proper functioning?

Ethical food

Happy eating, for me, is also about choosing food that is sustainably and ethically produced. This means local, organic produce that doesn't harm the environment, cause avoidable cruelty or suffering for animals, or cheat people out of their livelihood. It is awesome not to eat loads of the sugary, trans-fat-laden rubbish that passes as food, but if we buy our eggs from featherless chooks pinned in cages, or our asparagus has come 14,000 kilometres on a plane from Mexico, or 22 other sea creatures died in the catch to get that one fish we're eating, it can kind of spoil the whole effect. Food that is kind to the planet is kind to you.

Read the label

These days there's some pretty smart marketing out there to make you think that things are healthy. Sugar, for example, can have many names (sucrose, glucose, fructose, maltose, dextrose, corn syrup, etc.). And if you are avoiding dairy you'll need to look out for words like lactose, galactose, casein and whey. Even healthy options like nut milks will often have sugar, oil (usually canola) and salt added. If you are buying something in a jar, box or packet my first tip is to pick it up and read the label; if there's a truckload of ingredients in there and long lists of numbers that remind you of a Year 11 chemistry class, then pop it back down. That's not the stuff you want in your body.

Planning meals

Being an organisation nerd is really handy when it comes to happy eating. I love getting everything sorted and feeling inspired about the week ahead. In fact, Sunday is my shopping and prepping day; I buy all of my goodies for the week, then I make batches of things like paleo bread or protein balls and freeze them. I also freeze chicken or meat in portions, ready to take out and thaw later in the week. In the winter months I'll make stock, bone broth and hearty soups, freezing leftovers for later. In the summertime it's usually fresh salads served with a nice hit of protein.

Planning meals and preparing some or all of the ingredients ahead of time really helps you to stay on track with healthy food choices. It means that when you get home from work too exhausted to create a meal from scratch, you've got something ready to go.

Mindful eating

Eating is such a primal experience for us that we often do it on autopilot, shovelling in the food without really tasting it. Even worse, many of us eat while watching television or doing social media stuff on our smart phone, which means we often eat too fast, or overeat because we're not paying attention to what we're doing. Mindful eating is the practice of bringing your attention back to the present moment and noticing what you are doing, thinking and feeling, and studies show that it actually helps prevent overeating and assists with weight loss. (See page 185 for more about mindfulness.)

How I bring mindfulness to cooking and eating

* I play chilled music as I prepare the meal.
* When I sit down to eat, I make sure that I'm comfy and that there are no distractions from screens (large or small).
* I breathe in the aroma of the meal, and notice the colours and shapes of the ingredients.
* I slowly pick up my cutlery then take a small forkful or spoonful. I chew it slowly, savouring all of the flavours and textures. (When I first started mindful eating, I used to keep my eyes shut for this part so that I could really focus on the taste and feel of the food.)
* Afterwards, I have a moment of gratitude. I think how fortunate I am to be able to buy these ingredients and that I'm healthy enough to create this meal. I figure there are loads of people who don't have access to the abundance of healthy food that we have, and I never want to take that for granted.
* And then I clean up. I love to hand-wash dishes, pots and pans. It's quite meditative, and if I'm cooking with someone it's actually lovely to stand side by side and chat away. It doesn't even feel like I'm doing a chore!

My day on a plate

'What do you eat?' is one of the most common questions I am asked. The truth is that it changes a lot depending on where I am and how much travelling I'm doing, but it always includes brekkie, lunch, dinner and some kind of snack, plus at least 2 litres of water (very important – I'm always guzzling down water). Here's how a typical day might go.

8AM: Get up and do my yoga, then come home and make a green smoothie from baby spinach, frozen banana, a handful of macadamia nuts, almond milk, cinnamon, chia seeds and a few drops of stevia.

10AM: Catch up on my emails for a few hours, then have a handful of raw chocolate mixed with pecans and brazil nuts (I go through phases with nuts but always try to mix them up).

12PM: Go to a briefing for a media yoga class I am hosting and try one of their homemade raw energy balls – delish! (Actually, I might have two of them!)

2PM: On the way home, I grab a healthy salad from a local health-food store where they use heaps of fresh ingredients and the dressings are very whole-foodie – no nasties or numbers. (I'm a bit of detective when it comes to eating out and grabbing takeaway; I'm that person who researches the menu and asks a zillion questions.)

3PM: Have coconut water in the afternoon.

6PM: Make crispy salmon with kale, sweet spud and a simple avo mash.

8PM: Do more emails and have a little bit more raw chocolate.

THROUGHOUT THE DAY: I drink about 2.5 litres of water.

Brekkie is hands-down my favourite meal of the day. I've never skipped it, even when I've been on a crack-of-dawn flight and not feeling hungry. That's because I know how important it is from a health perspective. This is the meal that kickstarts your metabolism, fires up your neurochemistry and gets your digestion humming along. If you eat a nutrient-dense meal you feel good, you're focused and you're all set up for the day ahead. And I love how there are so many options: you can go sweet or savoury, make a smoothie if you're on the run or have a bowl of homemade Bircher muesli that you've soaked overnight. Sometimes I even have leftover dinner for brekkie if I'm in a savoury mood! There are no rules here; it's all about preparing something you love that nourishes you.

Apple pie might sound a bit 'treaty' to have first-up, but don't be fooled — it's delicious *and* healthy! You can use any kind of nut milk or even water for this recipe. Coconut milk is especially yummy.

APPLE PIE oats in a jar

- ½ cup rolled oats
- 2 cups almond milk
- 1 granny smith apple, cored and chopped into 2 cm pieces (keep the skin on for added health benefits)
- ¼ teaspoon ground nutmeg
- ½ teaspoon ground cinnamon, plus extra to serve
- ¼ teaspoon ground allspice
- 1 teaspoon maple syrup, plus extra to serve
- chopped walnuts, activated if possible (see page 10), to serve

Combine all of the ingredients except the walnuts in a saucepan and bring to the boil over a medium heat. Reduce the heat and simmer until the oats are cooked and the apple is nice and soft (about 5 minutes).

Spoon the porridge mixture into two jars and top with some walnuts, a pinch of cinnamon and a drizzle of maple syrup. This is best served warm, but you can eat it cold, too. (Which is great if you need to take your brekkie to work!)

Serves 2

This is a beautiful porridge with fairytale qualities that will bring a bit of magic to your morning. It's so satisfying and nourishing, too. You can substitute the pecans with pretty much any nut. Try walnuts, pistachios, almonds or macadamias. Make up a double batch and keep them for snacks and for toppings on yoghurt, muffins and cakes, as well as porridge. (To be honest, I tend not to make big batches – I might eat them all!)

GINGERBREAD porridge with candied pecans

½ cup rolled oats

2–3 cm piece of ginger, peeled and grated (or ½ teaspoon ground ginger)

½ teaspoon ground cinnamon

¼ teaspoon ground nutmeg

pinch of ground cloves

tiny pinch of salt flakes

1 cup almond milk, plus an extra ½ cup if needed

1 tablespoon maple syrup

Candied pecans

1 cup pecans, activated if possible (see page 10)

1 tablespoon coconut oil melted with 1 tablespoon maple syrup

¼ teaspoon ground cinnamon

tiny pinch of salt flakes

To make the candied pecans, heat the oven to 180°C and line a baking tray with baking paper. Spread the pecans over the prepared tray. Add the remaining ingredients and mix with your hands (it's the best way to add love to your meals) until the pecans are well coated. Bake for about 15 minutes, or until the house is filled with the aroma of maple syrup. Remove from the oven and allow to cool a little.

Place the oats, ginger, spices, salt, almond milk and maple syrup in a saucepan over a medium heat. Bring to the boil then reduce the heat and simmer for about 5 minutes, or until the oats are cooked. Transfer to serving bowls and top with a few candied pecans. Store leftover pecans in an airtight container in the pantry.

Serves 2

For many people, 'risotto' means a creamy, savoury rice dish, but this risotto is like no other you've tasted. It's creamy, yes, but it's also sweet and just brimming with nutrients and good fats to keep you going until lunch. (It also makes a brilliant dessert.) If you use frozen raspberries, just throw them on top (no need to thaw) – they will add a lovely crunch! You can use almond milk instead of coconut milk if you prefer.

quinoa chocolate RISOTTO

- ½ cup quinoa, rinsed
- 1 cup coconut milk, plus ½ cup extra if needed
- 1 tablespoon coconut oil
- 1 tablespoon cacao powder
- 1 tablespoon maple syrup (or honey, coconut nectar, rice malt syrup or sweetener of your choice)

To serve

- raspberries, fresh or frozen
- desiccated or shredded coconut

Place the quinoa, coconut milk and coconut oil in a saucepan over a medium heat and bring to the boil. Reduce the heat and stir in the cacao and sweetener. Cover and simmer for 20–25 minutes, or until the quinoa has sprouted little 'tails' and has tripled in size. Add a little more coconut milk (up to ½ cup) if the quinoa absorbs the liquid too quickly.

Transfer to serving bowls and top with the fresh or frozen raspberries and the coconut.

Serves 2

I have to admit, when I was recipe testing, this was the first one on my list. I mean, carrot cake *and* pancakes? Can it get any better than that? If you are trying stevia for the first time, don't overdo it – it's 300 times sweeter than sugar and has a really bitter aftertaste if you add too much. Also, raw, activated almonds (see page 10) are the healthiest way to go, though feel free to use roasted almonds if you prefer the crunch.

carrot cake PALEO PANCAKES

- 2 cups almond meal
- 1 teaspoon baking powder
- 3 eggs, lightly beaten
- 1½ cups almond milk
- 2 carrots, grated
- seeds of ½ vanilla pod (or ¼ teaspoon vanilla powder)
- ¼ cup sultanas
- ½ teaspoon ground cinnamon, plus extra to serve
- ¼ teaspoon ground nutmeg
- 3 drops of stevia (or 2 tablespoons maple syrup or honey)
- 3 tablespoons coconut oil

To serve

- almond butter
- coconut ice cream or coconut yoghurt
- ½ cup almonds, activated if possible (see page 10)
- maple syrup (optional)

Pop the almond meal and baking powder in a bowl and give it a good stir. Add everything else except the coconut oil and give it a really thorough mix, making sure you smooth out all the lumps.

Heat 2 teaspoons of the coconut oil in a frying pan over a medium heat. Add ¼ cup of the mixture to the pan, tilting it so it swirls over the base if you like a thinner pancake. Cook for 3 minutes, or until there are a few air bubbles in the centre and the edges are getting crispy. Flip it over and cook the other side for 1–3 minutes, depending on the thickness. Remove from the pan then set aside and keep warm. Repeat with the remaining pancake mixture.

To serve, top each pancake with a teaspoon of almond butter, a big dollop of coconut ice cream or yoghurt (yes please!), a few almonds, a sprinkle of cinnamon and, if you're a sweet tooth like me, a drizzle of maple syrup.

Serves 4

STICKY DATE
pancakes with coconut yoghurt

As you've probably guessed by now, I'm a huge fan of sweet brekkies, and this one definitely hits the spot. If you want to mix your pancake batter in a food processor, just whack in all of the ingredients (minus the dates) and whiz until smooth. Then stir in the dates and continue with the rest of the recipe.

2 ½ cups buckwheat flour

½ teaspoon ground cinnamon

pinch of salt flakes

3 cups almond milk

2 eggs, beaten

6 medjool dates, finely sliced, plus extra for serving

coconut oil, for frying

To serve

coconut yoghurt

chia seeds

maple syrup

Sift the flour, cinnamon and salt into a large bowl. Using a wooden spoon, make a well in the centre. Gradually add the almond milk, stirring in little circles to coax the flour away from the sides of the well (this helps make a smoother batter). Fold in the eggs and dates and mix thoroughly (try to separate any clumped date pieces so their awesomeness is spread evenly throughout the mixture). Pop the mixture into the fridge for at least 30 minutes if you like (it's supposed to give the starch time to absorb the moisture), but I'm always too hungry to wait and tend to dive straight into cooking my pancakes!

Heat a dab of coconut oil in a frying pan over a medium heat. Add ¼ cup of batter (or whatever amount suits you) and either swirl the pan to spread the batter over the base or, if you prefer thicker pancakes, leave it as is. Cook for 2–3 minutes, or until you see air bubbles in the centre of the pancake and the edges are starting to crisp. Flip and cook for another minute. Set aside and keep warm, then repeat with the remaining batter.

Divide the pancakes between serving plates and top with a scoop of coconut yoghurt, a sprinkle of chia seeds, half a date and a drizzle of maple syrup – the perfect Sunday brekkie!

Serves 4

TIPS

You can cook your pancakes in organic butter if you don't mind a bit of dairy (it makes them lovely and crispy on the edges).

Or to make them vegan, simply ditch the eggs – the pancakes still come up a treat.

I've tried a lot of crumbles in my time, but I must say the best recipe goes to an ex-boyfriend's mum, Julie Dignum. It was her idea to add macadamia nuts and oats to the yummy topping. Thanks, Jules!

6 granny smith apples, cored and cut into 2 cm dice (keep the skin on for extra chewiness)

1 punnet (125 g) blueberries (or ¾ cup frozen blueberries)

juice of 1 lemon

seeds of 1 vanilla pod (or ½ teaspoon vanilla powder)

2 teaspoons ground cinnamon

½ teaspoon ground nutmeg

Topping

1 cup almond meal

1 cup hazelnut meal

1 cup rolled oats

2 tablespoons coconut sugar

½ cup melted coconut oil

½ cup chopped macadamia nuts, activated if possible (see page 10)

coconut yoghurt or coconut ice cream, to serve

Preheat the oven to 180°C.

Place the apples and blueberries in a baking dish with the lemon juice, vanilla, cinnamon and nutmeg. Use your hands to mix the fruit, making sure it is evenly coated in the juice and spices.

To make the topping, combine the nut meals, oats, coconut sugar, coconut oil and nuts in a separate bowl and mix well until the ingredients start to clump together like 'oaty sand' (if that makes sense!).

Spoon the topping evenly over the apple and blueberry mixture and bake for 40 minutes, or until the apples are golden and bubbling. Serve warm with coconut yoghurt for breakfast or coconut ice cream for dessert.

Serves 6

TIP
You can replace the oats with another cup of almond meal if you prefer, or 1 cup of shredded coconut for extra crumbliness.

I love the aroma of freshly baked banana bread. It takes me back to my very first job at Brumby's Bakery! And this one is a beauty. It is especially delicious spread with almond butter, though of course you can use your favourite nut butter.

paleo banana and CRANBERRY BREAD

- 1 cup quinoa flour, sifted
- ½ cup coconut flour, sifted
- 1 cup almond meal
- 1½ teaspoons baking powder
- ½ teaspoon bicarbonate of soda
- pinch of salt flakes
- ½ teaspoon ground cinnamon
- 2 eggs
- 6 very ripe bananas
- ½ cup chopped medjool dates
- ½ cup dried cranberries, preferably unsweetened, plus extra to sprinkle on top
- seeds of 1 vanilla pod (or ½ teaspoon vanilla powder)
- ¼ cup coconut oil, melted, plus extra for greasing

Preheat the oven to 180°C and grease a loaf tin with a little coconut oil.

In a large mixing bowl combine the sifted flours, almond meal, baking powder, bicarb soda, salt and cinnamon.

In a separate bowl, whisk the eggs, then add the bananas, mashing them up with a fork. Stir in the dates, cranberries, vanilla and melted coconut oil. Now pour the wet ingredients into the dry ingredients and mix them really well.

Scoop the mixture into the prepared tin and bake this bad boy for 30–40 minutes (if you like it a little bit soft in the middle) or 40–50 minutes if you prefer it cooked through (a skewer poked into the middle should come out clean). It'll be hard to resist, but allow the loaf to sit for 5 minutes before turning it out onto a wire rack. Slice and serve warm with almond butter – *so* good!

Makes 1 loaf

TIP
This loaf freezes really well. Slice it up first and place baking paper between the slices for easy thawing.

I recently discovered that the go-to paleo loaf recipe I've been using for years (see page 44) makes *brilliant* muffins! These are full of pumpkin and loads of other goodies, and coupled with kale nut butter are a match made in heaven. Of course, you can always serve them topped with almond butter and a dash of maple syrup for a sweeter version.

paleo pumpkin muffins with kale nut butter

¼ cup extra-virgin olive oil, plus extra for greasing

2 cups grated pumpkin (any kind; I use butternut)

1 cup grated zucchini, pressed in a clean tea towel to remove excess moisture

4 eggs

2 cups almond meal

1 cup hazelnut meal

2 teaspoons baking powder

pinch of salt flakes

pinch of nutmeg

¼ cup pumpkin seeds

Kale nut butter

2 cups roughly chopped kale leaves, stalks removed

1 cup basil leaves

½ cup macadamia nuts, activated if possible (see page 10) roughly chopped

½ cup extra-virgin olive oil, plus extra if needed

¼ cup pine nuts, lightly toasted

¼ cup grated parmesan or pecorino (optional)

3 garlic cloves, roughly chopped

½ teaspoon salt flakes

Preheat the oven to 160°C and grease two six-cup muffin trays with olive oil.

Place the pumpkin, zucchini, eggs and oil in a big bowl and mix really well (it should look like a gluggy mess!). Add the almond meal, hazelnut meal, baking powder, salt and nutmeg and give it another good mix, breaking up any lumps of nut flour. Spoon this amazing mixture evenly into the cups of your muffin tins and sprinkle the tops with pumpkin seeds. Bake for 35 minutes, then pierce one muffin with a skewer to see if it comes out clean. Depending on your oven, you might need to bake them for a further 10–20 minutes (retest after every 10 minutes). Remove from the oven and allow to cool slightly before turning out onto a wire rack.

While the muffins are cooling, make the kale nut butter. Place all of the ingredients in a food processor and pulse until well combined. This is more like a pesto, really, so add a little more olive oil, if necessary, to get the consistency you prefer.

Once your muffins are cool enough to eat, serve with the kale nut butter.

Makes 12

TIPS
Store leftover nut butter in a sealed container in the fridge. It'll keep for 3-4 days, or longer if you omit the parmesan. (Pour a thin layer of olive oil on top to reduce oxidisation.)

Also, the muffins freeze really well. Simply pop them in zip-lock bags or freezer-proof containers. They will be good for at least 3 months.

This paleo loaf is easy to make and super versatile. You can serve it as a healthy breakfast with a savoury spread, as I've done here, or top it with some mashed avo and sliced cherry tomatoes (an old favourite of mine) for lunch, or spread it with nut butter and have it as a snack on the run.

PUMPKIN and zucchini loaf with minty ricotta spread

- 2 cups grated pumpkin (any kind; I use butternut)
- 1 cup grated zucchini, rolled in a clean tea towel to squeeze out excess moisture
- 4 eggs
- ¼ cup extra-virgin olive oil
- 1 cup almond meal
- 2 cups hazelnut meal
- pinch of salt flakes
- 2 teaspoons baking powder
- ¼ cup roughly chopped blanched almonds

Minty ricotta spread

- 1 cup ricotta
- 1 bunch of mint, leaves picked and finely chopped (½ cup loosely packed leaves)
- zest and juice of ½ lemon
- salt flakes and freshly ground black pepper

Preheat the oven to 160°C and line a loaf tin with baking paper. Place the pumpkin, zucchini, eggs and oil in a large bowl and mix thoroughly. Add the almond meal, hazelnut meal, salt and baking powder and give it another good mix, breaking up any lumps. Spoon the mixture into the prepared tin and sprinkle over the almonds. Bake for 1 hour, then test with a skewer. If the skewer comes out covered with sticky mixture, return the loaf to the oven for another 20–25 minutes. Allow to cool completely before removing from the tin.

To make the minty ricotta spread, combine all of the ingredients in a small bowl and stir well. Slice the loaf and spread with the minty ricotta for a delishimo breakfast or snack!

Makes 1 loaf

TIPS
This paleo bread is also delicious with Kale Nut Butter (see page 42), and it freezes really well (up to 3 months).

Simply slice it up and freeze it in zip-locks. (You can place baking paper between the slices if you like; it makes separating them easier.)

Since moving to Sydney, I've really fallen in love with brekkie salads — a popular menu item here. Once you try this recipe, you'll understand why! You can also serve this salad with fried eggs or with halved hard-boiled eggs (which you can cook the day before and store in the fridge in their shells).

brekkie salad with poached egg

- 1 cup finely sliced kale, stalks removed
- ½ cup finely chopped broccoli (it should look a bit like green couscous)
- 1 avocado, sliced or diced
- 1 cup baby spinach leaves
- 2 tablespoons chopped coriander leaves
- 1 tablespoon chopped mint leaves
- ½ cup roughly chopped almonds, activated if possible (see page 10)
- ¼ cup goji berries
- 2 eggs
- 2 teaspoons apple cider vinegar

Dressing

- 2 tablespoons almond butter
- 2 tablespoons extra-virgin olive oil
- juice of 1 lemon
- salt flakes and freshly ground black pepper, to taste

In a large bowl, toss together the kale, broccoli, avocado, spinach, herbs, almonds and berries.

To make the dressing, place the ingredients in a small screw-top jar with 2 tablespoons of water and give it a good shake, adding a little more oil if you like it runnier. Pour over the salad and toss well. Divide the salad between serving plates and set aside.

Now for the eggs. Loads of people tell me they struggle with poaching eggs, and for a long time I was one of them. But I've learned a few tricks. First of all, fill a saucepan with water to a depth of 10 cm and add the apple cider vinegar. (The vinegar helps prevent the egg white from spreading.) Pop on the lid and place the pan over a high heat to bring to the boil. Crack one egg (I reckon it's best to do one at a time) into a cup or little bowl. When the water is boiling, remove the lid and reduce the heat to medium. Grab a spoon and carefully swirl the water in a circle to create a little whirlpool, then slide the egg into the centre of the whirlpool (holding the cup close to the water). Cook the egg for 3–4 minutes (for a soft yolk), then remove it with a slotted spoon. Pop it on one of the serving plates, then repeat with the remaining egg.

Finish with one last sprinkle of salt and pepper, and away you go!

Serves 2

You may have heard of red shakshuka (a traditional Middle Eastern dish of eggs poached in a pan with crushed tomato, onion and chillies). I created this green version for times when I really want to jumpstart my day. It actually makes a brilliant lunch or dinner, too – jam-packed full of nutrients, and so tasty!

GREEN shakshuka

2 tablespoons extra-virgin olive oil
1 onion, diced
1 garlic clove, diced
1 teaspoon ground cumin
1 teaspoon ground coriander
2 cups finely chopped broccoli florets
3 big handfuls of baby spinach leaves

4 eggs
½ cup (100 g) crumbled feta
½ avocado, diced
handful of micro coriander shoots (or any edible micro herb or petal)
salt flakes and freshly ground black pepper

Heat the oil in a large frying pan over a medium heat. Add the onion and garlic and sauté for 2–3 minutes, or until the onion is translucent. Stir in the spices and cook for 1 minute. Add the broccoli and sauté for 1 minute or until it turns bright green (it might take longer depending on how finely you chop it). Add the spinach and stir it around for 1 minute, or until it just begins to wilt. Now make four little indentations in the mixture and crack an egg into each one. Cook for 5 minutes or until the eggs are poached. (Pop a lid on for 1–2 minutes if you want to speed things up.)

Remove from the heat, sprinkle over the feta, avocado and herbs, and season with salt and pepper. Tuck in!

Serves 2

TIP
I use goat's milk feta, but you can use whatever type you like: sheep's milk feta, cow's milk feta or a mix.

I'm well and truly into salmon, not only for its umami flavour but also for its amazing omega-3s, which are crucial for cardiovascular and brain health, among other things. This recipe is super quick and easy because it uses smoked salmon. Try to get fresh dill if you can, but don't worry if you can't. Instead, use 1 teaspoon of dill flakes in the omelette mixture and serve with a sprinkle of chopped parsley, chives, chervil or whatever fresh herb you have to hand.

salmon, kale and dill OMELETTE

5 eggs

¼ cup almond milk

2 cups chopped kale leaves (stalks removed)

small handful of dill, chopped (save a few sprigs for the top)

salt flakes and freshly ground black pepper

2 tablespoons extra-virgin olive oil, plus extra to serve

60 g smoked salmon, sliced

½ cup crumbled feta

Combine the eggs, almond milk, kale, dill and seasoning in a bowl and give them a good old mix-up.

Heat 1 tablespoon of the oil in a frying pan over a medium heat. Pour in half of the egg mixture and cook for 1–2 minutes, or until the base has firmed up but the top is still gooey. Arrange half of the salmon and feta on one side of the omelette and fold the other side over the top (or place the salmon and feta in the middle of the omelette and fold four edges into the centre like an envelope). Cook for a further minute (pop the lid on the pan if you like), or until the salmon and feta are heated through.

Remove from the pan and keep warm while you repeat with the remaining egg mixture, salmon and feta.

Serve with a drizzle of olive oil and a few dill sprigs.

Serves 2

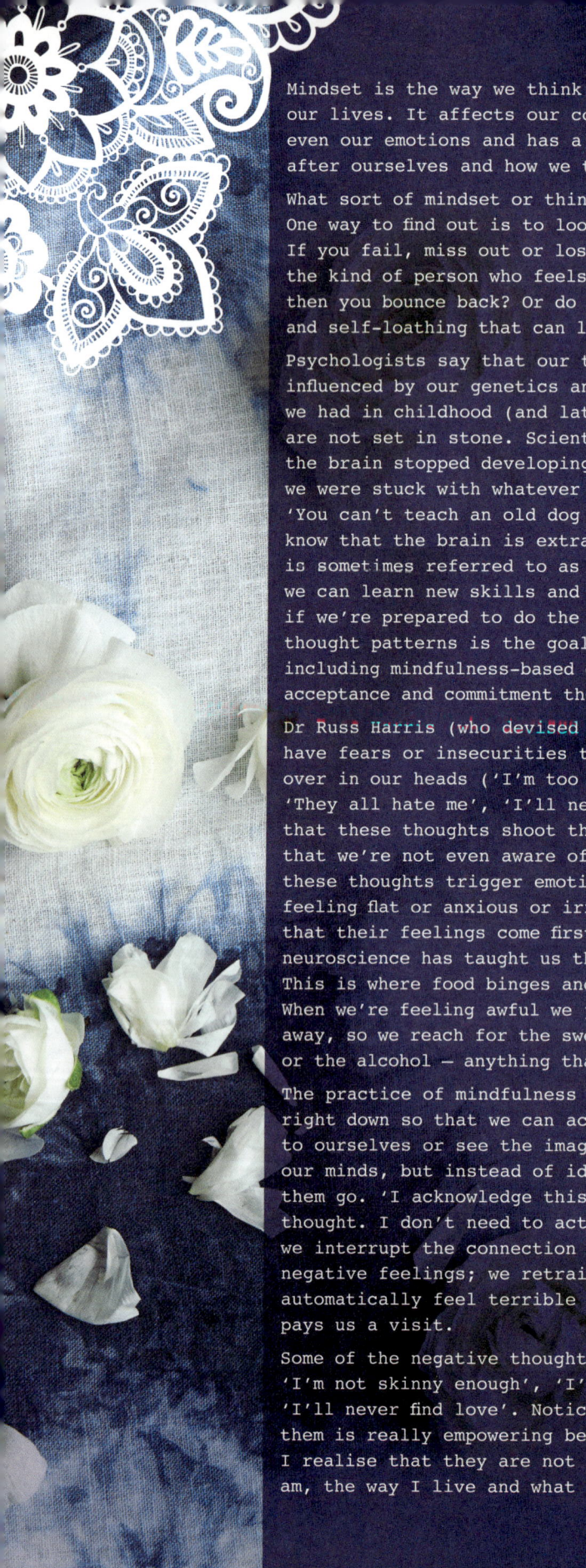

Mindset is the way we think about things that happen in our lives. It affects our confidence, our resilience and even our emotions and has a huge influence on how we look after ourselves and how we treat others.

What sort of mindset or thinking patterns do you have? One way to find out is to look at how you cope with stress. If you fail, miss out or lose something or someone, are you the kind of person who feels sad for a little while but then you bounce back? Or do you fall into a pit of despair and self-loathing that can last days or even weeks?

Psychologists say that our thinking patterns are partly influenced by our genetics and partly by the experiences we had in childhood (and later), but that these patterns are not set in stone. Scientists used to believe that the brain stopped developing in adolescence and that we were stuck with whatever we had (like that saying, 'You can't teach an old dog new tricks'). But we now know that the brain is extraordinarily malleable (this is sometimes referred to as 'neuroplasticity'), and that we can learn new skills and create new synaptic pathways if we're prepared to do the work. Changing unhelpful thought patterns is the goal of many talking therapies, including mindfulness-based cognitive therapies like acceptance and commitment therapy (ACT).

Dr Russ Harris (who devised ACT) says that most of us have fears or insecurities that keep playing over and over in our heads ('I'm too fat', 'I'm not good enough', 'They all hate me', 'I'll never find a partner'), but that these thoughts shoot through our minds so fast that we're not even aware of them. The problem is that these thoughts trigger emotions, and we can find ourselves feeling flat or anxious or irritated. (Some people think that their feelings come first and then their thoughts, but neuroscience has taught us that it's the other way around.) This is where food binges and other addictions come in. When we're feeling awful we just want the feeling to go away, so we reach for the sweet stuff, the fatty foods, or the alcohol — anything that gives us a high.

The practice of mindfulness helps us to slow our thoughts right down so that we can actually hear what we're saying to ourselves or see the images that are passing through our minds, but instead of identifying with them, we let them go. 'I acknowledge this thought, but it's just a thought. I don't need to act upon it.' The idea is that we interrupt the connection between negative thoughts and negative feelings; we retrain our brains so that we don't automatically feel terrible if one of our old thoughts pays us a visit.

Some of the negative thoughts I've worked through include 'I'm not skinny enough', 'I'm not pretty enough' and 'I'll never find love'. Noticing them and working through them is really empowering because at the end of the day I realise that they are not 'me'. I get to choose who I am, the way I live and what I stand for.

MIND

> Work with the mind, and the body follows.
>
> Byron Katie, author and speaker

emotional EATING

I'd be lying if I said that my health is never affected by my emotions. At times, especially if I feel super stressed, exhausted or sad, I can still overindulge, which for me means demolishing a whole block of raw chocolate or a couple of gluten-free brownies. This is the first step in the binge cycle, and we've all been there. The problem is, sugary foods only give you a rush for about five minutes, then you get the insulin spike and energy crash that leave you feeling worse than you did before, especially if you're like me and pile a whole load of guilt on top as well. It's at this point that most people will reach for more sugar, and so the cycle continues and the weight slowly creeps up. Fortunately, I have some little strategies I use to break the cycle.

How to cope with a binge

* 'Change the channel': go for a walk or bike ride, see a movie – anything to take your mind away from food.
* Call a mate and talk it through.
* Take a power nap (exhaustion is a trigger for bingeing): you'll wake up feeling refreshed, like someone has hit the reset button.
* Find the trigger: if something is stressing you out, see what you can do to reduce that stress.
* Try not to beat yourself up about it. Making mistakes is part of the journey; we all do it. You're not alone. And anyway, you can start again tomorrow!
* Book an appointment with your doctor or counsellor (if you have one); you'll feel better having taken the first step.

Asking for help

When I was younger, I used to think that asking for help for emotional problems was a sign of weakness. I didn't want to admit that I couldn't fix everything by myself. Now I totally understand that it's actually a sign of strength. It takes courage to say 'I need a little help here'. And the beautiful thing is that you find out how amazing, generous and kind people are.

I've seen a counsellor or a psychologist on and off over the years, and I plan to keep seeing one whenever I feel the need for a 'check-up from the neck up'. I've learned that there's not much point putting all that effort into being fit and healthy when my state of mind can easily undo all my hard work!

If you're new to the idea of therapy, ask your doctor or a close friend for some recommendations. It'll feel a bit strange at first, but please try to give the therapist or counsellor a few goes – it takes time to get your story out and for you to get to know each other. I'd stick with it for at least four sessions before you decide whether it's working for you or not. Sometimes you might need to try a couple of different therapists before you find the right one, and that's totally fine.

CONFIDENCE

For years I thought I was fat, and like many people who are self-critical and judgemental, I turned to food to make me feel better, which meant I put on more weight. So I'd diet, and feel awesome for a bit, but then something negative would happen in my life and the weight would pile on again. This yoyo dieting was exhausting, and staying healthy felt like an uphill battle. Then one day I thought, 'You know what? I'm a healthy and fit girl!' And then every time my mind would try to say 'I'm fat', I would consciously replace it with 'I'm healthy and fit'. This took a lot of practice, and mindfulness really helped, but once I understood the power of positive self-talk, I've never looked back.

The turning point for me was realising my personal responsibility, that it was all up to me. I had to make a choice: 'Today I choose to be kind to my body.' I know that makes it sound simple, but it's not. It's an ongoing process. Every day I choose to nurture my body and soul. Of course, even now, some days are a struggle. If I'm feeling low, it can take great discipline to steer myself away from sweet food, or if I'm really tired after work, to make myself go to the gym. But every time I choose a nurturing action, it becomes a little easier. And it will work this way for you, too. Just don't be so hard on yourself if you slip up. It's okay to make crappy choices now and again. Just know that you can begin now.

If you want to be the fittest, healthiest version of you, then honour yourself on every level. Nothing changes until you change your mindset, until you trust yourself and let go of what other people think of you.

One little trick to use is to start each day with a positive affirmation like 'I am going to make this day amazing!' Just say it to yourself, no one else needs to know about it – and then go on your merry way. If something tough comes up, remember that you promised yourself today would be amazing. So don't let yourself down. Every morning I tell myself that I'm going to show up and give it my very best, whatever happens. It reminds me that I can't control everything that happens to me, but I can control how I respond. It works for me. Try it on.

Assertiveness

Confident people are also assertive. They are comfortable expressing their opinions without dominating the conversation and will speak up when they know something is not right. They're not rude or aggressive; they simply believe that their opinion is just as important as everyone else's. And it is!

That said, assertiveness has always been tricky for me. I love to deliver my best and keep everyone happy, so if something doesn't feel right I find it challenging to speak up because I don't like conflict. But the reality is you don't grow from being comfortable – you grow from getting outside your comfort zone.

The old saying 'You can't please all of the people all of the time' (or even some of the time) is pretty accurate. First of all, there will be lots of people who will not like you no matter what you do. It's the same for all of us. And you might not like them, either, so don't worry about them. This doesn't mean you have to be mean to them; just don't go out of your way to please them. Meanwhile, the people who do care (your real friends and your family) are quietly waiting for you to assert yourself. Honestly, each time you speak to them they are probably wishing that you'd tell them what you really think! And yes, other people might get their feathers ruffled when you speak up, but that's their problem, not yours.

You are a valuable person and trying to shrink yourself down so that you don't offend people doesn't help anyone, least of all you. People will respect you more if you assert yourself. As the saying goes, 'Speak the truth, even if your voice shakes'.

Tips on being more assertive

If you feel uncomfortable expressing your opinions and sharing your ideas, lean into that feeling. It's normal. Know that you'll be okay.

Stop apologising. It actually makes the other person feel uncomfortable, and if you do it a lot, they're probably also going to get annoyed with you.

If someone asks you for a 'favour' and you don't want to do it, simply say, 'I'm sorry, no'. Or if you are genuinely not sure, give yourself some time to reflect and say, 'Let me think about it, and I'll get back to you'. Keep your answer short and simple – you don't have to give a detailed explanation. You are a worthwhile human being with a right to express your own views and to take care of your own needs. If the person insists on an explanation or is angry, then you'll know you've dodged a bullet!

Practise saying 'no' in front of a mirror. Say it clearly and evenly – not in an aggressive tone, or in a timid, questioning tone. After you've got used to saying it, try it in a real situation where the stakes are not too high (for example, when you and your friends are deciding on which movie to see on the weekend).

RESILIENCE

People who have spent their whole careers researching happiness have found that resilience – the ability to bounce back from adversity and learn from our mistakes – is massively important. It might sound weird, but failure is one of my favourite topics. I mean, how would we learn anything if we didn't make mistakes? At the time we stuff up, we think that the world is crumbling around us, but when we look back, we can see that everything happens for a reason.

I have a lot of personal experience with failure, and I don't regret a second of it! I failed some of my exams at uni even though I was passionate about the subject and had worked really hard. If I hadn't failed, I would never have discovered that I'm a very visual learner and that I retain information way better with visual cues and presentations. I've lost TV and radio gigs, too, which in hindsight I'm really glad about because it meant I was free to take up other opportunities. It's amazing to look back and realise that these 'failures' actually made way for something more incredible.

Failure is just a label. When you try something and it doesn't work, you're not failing, you're *trying*, that's all. The experience has nothing to do with who you are as a person.

Tips on coping with failure

* First of all, drop the word failure: think of it as 'trying' or 'learning'. You're still the same person you were before you tried!

* Try to find the lesson in it and use it as an affirmation. For example, I did a screen test for a television show last year but didn't get the gig, so my affirmation was 'I love working in TV and I'm going to get some more experience under my belt'.

* Whenever you start thinking 'I'm a failure', find three reasons to prove the opposite – that you are great at lots of things and you're doing perfectly fine. And they don't have to be big showy reasons, either. The more specific you are, the better. 'I'm good at staying in touch with my friends', 'I'm good at cooking', 'I'm good at answering the phone'. Once you find a couple of these, it'll open your mind and you'll find stacks of proof that you're an amazing human being!

* Try not to wallow in negative feelings. The experience is over, and there's nothing you can do to change that. It's out of your control. Some people have such a hard time letting go of the past that they become sick and miserable. It's not bad to want to achieve, but if it's making you depressed, you need to shift your focus. Do things that you know you're good at for a while. When you feel your confidence growing again, get up, dust yourself off and focus on the next thing.

VALUES

Defining your values is a key step in becoming clear on what you want your life to look like. Values are the standards we live by — the beliefs we hold about what is worthwhile and important. Our values influence our attitudes, which in turn guide our actions. Integrity is when our actions match our values.

Experts say that if we live according to core values that focus on personal growth and connection with others, we are much more likely to be happy. Conversely, people who place a higher value on extrinsically based goals, such as wealth and status, have higher rates of depression, anxiety and melancholy.

What do you value? Here are some ideas to consider: courage, honesty, wisdom, passion, balance, peace, justice, connection to others, security, sharing, reliability, wealth, vision, honesty, unity and structure. Make a list of your five most important values and write them in the box below, then keep these values close.

My top 5 values

1.
2.
3.
4.
5.

My core values

Love: To love myself and everyone who comes into my life and to be open to the love of others.

Vitality: To be the healthiest version of myself – it brings me happiness from the inside.

Vision: To let myself dream big.

Tenacity: To have the clarity and drive to realise my dreams no matter how far out they seem.

Hard work: To do what needs to be done with enthusiasm, energy and commitment; when I love what I do, it's all flow.

GRATITUDE

We all go through tough times; it's part of the journey. We all feel disappointment or resentment when things don't turn out the way we hoped; when we fail at something or we miss out. For most of us, though, the toughest times involve losing someone we love – through death, relationship breakdown or even just geographical separation. At those times the grief can be so overwhelming that it can take weeks, months or even years to recover our old spark.

I'd be lying if I said my life has been all peachy, but I feel really lucky that I've had great souls around me who have loved and supported me through the tough times. And you know what? Those rough patches have helped me get to the core of who I am and what I value.

Feeling sad is a normal and necessary part of the grieving process, but hanging on to your grief and defining yourself as 'that person whose partner died' or 'that girl whose partner cheated on her with her best friend' is only going to keep you stuck in a sad place. People think that the more tears we shed, the more it proves how much we loved the person we lost. But if you think about it, we're not crying for the other person (they don't want our tears, or even need them – especially if they're dead!), we're crying because we're angry about being dumped or we're frightened of being alone.

It's all about flipping our thought patterns so that we try to see that everything happens for a good reason – people come, people go, it's all good. And one way I have learned to do this is by being grateful, by focusing on the positives in any situation. I've been doing this for years now, and it's amazing! It's changed my whole mindset. When something happens that used to make me feel 'let down', I don't focus on what I've lost, but on what I've gained.

Tips on showing gratitude

* When you thank someone, look into their eyes and say it from the heart.
* Send a thank-you card to someone.
* Start a gratitude book, and at the end of each day, write down five things you're grateful for, no matter how big or small.
* At the dinner table, take turns talking about something that went well today.

I love these recipes — they're so nutrient-dense! You can feel them healing and nourishing you with every mouthful. Plus, for lots of them, you can make up batches to freeze so you're never short of a nutritious snack or meal, even when you're short on time. Being organised makes it loads easier to stick to healthy eating habits.

As with all of my recipes, please try to buy local or at least Australian-grown produce. And if you can't find an ingredient, don't panic — there'll always be something you can replace it with. So feel free to experiment, to mix things about to suit your tastebuds. You're the master of your own journey and that includes what you cook, so make these recipes work for you. Let them be a joy for you to prepare and share with the people you love to cook for.

sweet spud and kale bites with avocado dressing

I love this recipe because it is so versatile. You can munch these delicious morsels straight out of the oven, or eat them cold for lunch the next day. You can even break them up and toss them through a leafy green salad.

2 sweet potatoes, scrubbed and diced

1 bunch of kale, stalks removed and leaves very finely chopped (about 2 cups chopped kale)

½ red onion, very finely diced

1 garlic clove, crushed

½ teaspoon ground cumin

2 tablespoons full-fat coconut cream

salt flakes and freshly ground black pepper

crushed pistachios, to serve

Avocado dressing

1 avocado

juice and zest of 1 lime

2 tablespoons extra-virgin olive oil

¼ teaspoon ground cumin

salt flakes and freshly ground black pepper

Preheat the oven to 180°C and line a baking tray with baking paper.

Meanwhile, steam the sweet potato in a double-boiler or a saucepan with a steamer insert for about 10 minutes, or until soft. Transfer to a large mixing bowl.

Add the kale to the steamed sweet potato and roughly mash, leaving a few chunks of spud. Add the onion, garlic, cumin, coconut cream, salt and pepper and stir until just combined. With wet hands, roll walnut-sized balls of the mixture and place them on the prepared tray. Bake for 15–20 minutes, or until they start to go a bit golden and crisp.

Meanwhile, to make the avocado dressing, use a food processor or handheld blender to puree all the ingredients until creamy.

Serve the bites drizzled with the dressing and topped with crushed pistachios.

Serves 3–4 as a snack

This slice is a cinch to make, and whether you have it as a snack or with a salad for lunch, it will keep you firing on all cylinders! Try making it on a Sunday so you've got snacks on hand for the coming week. It freezes well (place the squares between sheets of baking paper in zip-lock bags).

quinoa surprise SLICE

¼ cup extra-virgin olive oil, plus extra for greasing

4 tablespoons almond meal

1 sweet potato, scrubbed and diced

1 cup quinoa, rinsed

½ onion, finely chopped

2 garlic cloves, minced

2 thyme sprigs, leaves picked

1 rosemary sprig, leaves picked

½ bunch of kale, stalks removed and leaves finely chopped

¼ cup pitted kalamata olives, roughly chopped

2 large eggs, lightly beaten

½ cup (100 g) crumbled goat's milk feta

salt flakes and freshly ground black pepper

Preheat the oven to 180°C and line a baking tray with baking paper. Also, grease a 20 x 20 cm slice tin with a little olive oil and sprinkle 2 tablespoons of the almond meal over the base.

Spread the sweet potato on the prepared tray, then drizzle over 2 tablespoons of the olive oil, tossing the cubes so they are well coated. Bake for 15 minutes or until the sweet potato is soft and beginning to brown. Remove from the oven and set aside.

Meanwhile, place the rinsed quinoa in a saucepan with 2 cups of water. Cover and bring to the boil over a medium heat, then reduce the heat and simmer for 10 minutes, or until the quinoa has sprouted little tails and all the liquid has been absorbed.

Heat the remaining olive oil in a large saucepan over a medium heat. Add the onion, garlic, thyme and rosemary and cook for 2–3 minutes, or until fragrant. Now add the roasted sweet spud, cooked quinoa, kale and olives, and toss them around a bit to combine. Sprinkle over the remaining almond meal, then stir in the eggs, feta and a good grind of black pepper. Check the seasoning and add some more salt if you like, though the olives and feta are already pretty salty. Transfer the mixture to the prepared tin and bake for 45 minutes to 1 hour, or until the edges are nice and crispy. Allow to cool slightly before cutting into squares. Then take a moment to be thankful that you're able to create and enjoy such beautiful food with people you love!

Serves 4–6

These little muffins are delicious as a snack but also make a yummy breakfast. If you're not into dairy products you can leave out the feta. They also freeze really well. (Just thaw them and then reheat in the oven.)

mushroom, feta and pine nut MUFFINS

1 tablespoon extra-virgin olive oil, plus extra for greasing
1 onion, diced
1 garlic clove, finely chopped
2 cups chopped mushrooms (Swiss brown, button or portobello are all good)
1½ cups almond meal
1 teaspoon baking powder
4 large eggs
¼ cup almond milk
1 bunch of basil, leaves picked and finely chopped
½ cup (100 g) crumbled goat's milk feta
⅓ cup pine nuts (reserve 1 tablespoon to sprinkle on top)
salt flakes and freshly ground black pepper

Preheat the oven to 180°C. Grease a 12-cup muffin tray, or line it with patty cases.

Heat the olive oil in a frying pan over a medium heat. Add the onion and garlic and sauté for 2–3 minutes, or until the onion is translucent. Add the mushrooms and cook for 8–10 minutes, or until the onion is starting to caramelise and the mushrooms are a lovely dark colour. (Most of the liquid should have evaporated.) Remove from the heat and set aside.

Place the almond meal and baking powder in a large bowl and use a wooden spoon to make a little well in the centre. Crack the eggs into the well and give them a good old mix. Add the almond milk a little at a time, mixing in between additions. When the batter is nice and smooth, fold in the cooked mushroom mixture, chopped basil, feta and pine nuts and season to taste. Divide the mixture evenly between the muffin tray cups or patty cases. Bake for 20–25 minutes, or until a toothpick popped into the centre of one of the muffins comes out clean. Set aside to cool for 5 minutes before turning out onto a wire rack. Tuck in!

Makes 12

This spicy, cabbage-based dish has many of the flavours of traditional kimchi, but without the fermentation. I've always adored spicy food, and this dish fits right in there. It makes an amazing side for red meat.

cheat's KIMCHI

- 2 tablespoons good-quality sea salt
- ½ large wombok cabbage, shredded
- 1 tablespoon sesame seeds
- 3 tablespoons fish sauce
- 2 garlic cloves, minced
- 2 cm piece of ginger, grated
- 1 teaspoon cayenne pepper
- zest and juice of 1 lemon

Place 2 litres of water in a large stockpot over a high heat. Add the salt and bring to the boil. Add the cabbage and cook for just 3 minutes. Drain well, then transfer the cabbage to a large serving bowl.

Using a food processor or mortar and pestle, combine the sesame seeds, fish sauce, garlic, ginger, cayenne pepper and lemon zest and juice, and whiz or grind to form a paste. Spoon over the still-warm cabbage, stir well and serve immediately.

Serves 4–6 as a side

TIP
Wombok (often called Chinese cabbage) shouldn't be too hard to find, but if you can't get any, this dish is just as delicious with regular green cabbage.

It took me a while to cotton on to homemade sauerkraut (I was so in love with the organic store-bought stuff!), but now I'm hooked. It's just so easy to make yourself, and so much fun. If you love this version, try it with red cabbage. And if you don't like caraway, substitute with peppercorns, dill seeds, fenugreek or whatever takes your fancy.

I really encourage you to add some fermented food to your diet. The fermentation process produces friendly bacteria that are very beneficial for gut health and overall immune health. (See the section on fermented drinks on page 220 for further information).

This recipe needs to be started 3–10 days in advance, depending on how funky you like your sauerkraut.

SIMPLE sauerkraut

1 green cabbage (1 kg), cored and shredded (reserve a couple of outer leaves)

1 tablespoon good-quality sea salt

1–2 teaspoons caraway seeds (optional)

Place the shredded cabbage and salt in a large bowl and massage it with your hands (or use a pestle) until it starts to soften and give up its juices. This will take at least 5–10 minutes. (You can also cover it and leave it for half an hour before you begin massaging.)

When the cabbage is soft, mix in the caraway seeds, if using, then transfer to a 1-litre preserving jar (or two smaller jars). Press the cabbage down with the back of a spoon so that the juices rise up and it is fully submerged. Fold a piece of the reserved cabbage leaf to fit across the top and then weigh it down with a shot glass or a clean stone, making sure you leave 2–3 cm free at the top. Pop the lid on loosely, cover the jar with a tea towel and keep it in a warmish spot (near your fridge or your dryer if it's winter) for 3–5 days. (If it's summer, you might want to check it after the first day or so, as higher temperatures speed up the fermenting process.)

After 3 days, taste it and see what you think. The longer you leave it, the tangier the flavour will become. If you like a milder ferment, place it in the fridge after the first few days; if you like it strong and sour, leave it for at least 10 days before refrigerating. Just check it every couple of days, pressing it down with a spoon so that the gases escape and the cabbage remains submerged.

Makes a 1-litre jar

This pretty salad makes a lovely lunch and is perfect to take to a barbecue. I use the grater function on my food processor to shred all my slaw veggies, but you can also use a mandoline or a sharp knife. And if you can't get your hands on fresh blueberries, use a punnet of strawberries, hulled and cut in half – they will do the trick.

summer slaw with blueberries and homemade MAYO

- ¼ green cabbage, shredded
- ¼ red cabbage, shredded
- 2 carrots, grated
- 6 radishes, very finely sliced into rounds
- ½ red onion, finely sliced
- 2 punnets (250 g) fresh blueberries (not frozen)
- ½ bunch of coriander, leaves picked and chopped
- 1 tablespoon cumin seeds, toasted
- 1 cup Homemade Mayo (see recipe below)
- salt flakes and freshly ground black pepper

Homemade mayo

- 2 egg yolks
- 2 tablespoons lemon juice
- pinch each of salt flakes and freshly ground black pepper
- 2 cups extra-virgin olive oil

Place the cabbage, carrot, radish and onion in a large serving bowl and toss until well combined. Add the blueberries, coriander and cumin seeds and gently mix in.

To make the homemade mayo, use a handheld blender to whiz the egg yolks, lemon juice salt and pepper together in a small bowl or blender beaker. Then, with the motor still running, gradually add the olive oil in a thin stream until the mayo is creamy. (Or use a food processor if you prefer.) If the mixture is too thick, blend in 1 tablespoon of water.

Spoon the mayo onto the salad and give it a good mix. Season to taste, cover with plastic wrap and pop in the fridge to chill for 40–60 minutes.

Serves 4–6

Waldorf salads are real crowd-pleasers, but sometimes you can't be sure what's in the dressing (many commercial ones are full of dodgy oils, preservatives and sugar). So I make my own with homemade mayo. Making your own mayo is cheaper and bucketloads healthier, plus it tastes better!

kale waldorf salad with real mayo dressing

- ½ bunch of kale, stalks removed, leaves torn
- 1 apple, finely sliced (leave the skin on)
- 1 cup red grapes, halved lengthways
- 2 celery stalks, finely chopped
- 1 cup walnuts, activated if possible (see page 10)
- ½ cup raisins
- salt flakes and freshly ground black pepper

Waldorf dressing
- ⅓ cup Homemade Mayo (see recipe on page 81)
- 1 tablespoon wholegrain mustard
- 1 tablespoon lime juice
- pinch each of salt flakes and freshly ground black pepper

To make the dressing, combine the ingredients in a small bowl and mix well.

Now grab a big bowl and pop in the kale, apple, grapes, celery, walnuts and raisins. Add the dressing, season to taste, toss, then serve!

Serves 4–6

I once dated a fancy chef who, on our first date, said he'd make 'poached salmon with broccoli couscous and quinoa crunch'. I told him it sounded lovely but that I didn't eat couscous because it contains gluten (yes, I'm that girl who has all the crazy dietary requirements on a first date). He explained that the broccoli was the couscous, just chopped really finely. So as much as I'd love to claim the idea of broccoli couscous as my own, I have to credit my ex-boyfriend.

broccoli 'couscous' SALAD

- 1 head of broccoli
- 1 cup macadamia nuts, activated if possible (see page 10), roughly chopped (reserve 1 tablespoon to serve)
- handful of mint leaves, roughly chopped
- seeds of 1 pomegranate
- juice and zest of 1 lime
- 3 tablespoons extra-virgin olive oil
- salt flakes and freshly ground black pepper

Roughly chop the broccoli into big chunks and pulse in a food processor until it resembles couscous (or do it by hand with a sharp knife). Transfer to a large serving bowl along with the macadamias, mint, pomegranate seeds, lime juice and olive oil. Season to taste and give everything a good toss. Top with the reserved macadamia nuts and a nice hit of lime zest and tuck in!

Serves 4

TIPS
You can use any nut in this salad — almonds and cashews are brill. And if you can't find pomegranate seeds (don't forget you can freeze the seeds when they're in season), goji berries, cranberries, blueberries or even strawberries will work just as well. Experiment to find the perfect combo and enjoy!

RAINBOW yoga bowl with green hummus

I make this salad on my yoga days when I really want a rainbow of coloured veggies with all their cool phytonutrients (the health-boosting nutrients found in fruit and veggies). Ditch the eggs and you have a vegan delight.

1 sweet potato, scrubbed and cut into 2 cm pieces

1 tablespoon extra-virgin olive oil

pinch of paprika, plus extra to serve

salt flakes and freshly ground black pepper

1 head of broccoli, florets chopped

1 teaspoon black sesame seeds

2 handfuls of baby spinach leaves

10–12 cherry tomatoes, halved

1 avocado, sliced

½ cup Simple Sauerkraut (see recipe on page 78)

½ cup Green Hummus (see recipe below)

2 teaspoons apple cider vinegar

2 eggs

Green hummus

1 x 400 g can chickpeas, rinsed

handful of baby spinach leaves

2 cherry tomatoes

1 garlic clove, roughly chopped

2 tablespoons extra-virgin olive oil

1 tablespoon tahini

juice of 1 lemon

salt flakes and freshly ground black pepper

To serve

almond butter

pumpkin seeds

sunflower seeds

pinch of ground paprika

lemon wedges

Preheat the oven to 180°C.

Spread the sweet potato on a baking tray and drizzle over the olive oil. Add the paprika, salt and pepper, then rub the oil and spices into the potato until it's well coated. Roast for about 25 minutes or until the potato is crispy. Remove from the oven and set aside to cool.

Meanwhile, place the broccoli in a steamer over a medium heat and cook for 5 minutes or until it turns a lovely bright green. Remove from the heat and run under cold water to stop the cooking process (and retain the colour). Sprinkle with the sesame seeds and set aside.

To make the green hummus, place all of the ingredients in a food processor and whiz until nice and smooth.

To assemble your salad, take two serving bowls and place a handful of baby spinach in the base of each one to create a little pillow for all your other goodies. On top, in separate mounds, arrange the broccoli, tomatoes, avocado, sauerkraut, hummus and sweet potato.

For the poached eggs, place the apple cider vinegar and 10 cm of water in a saucepan over a high heat. Crack one egg into a teacup. When the water is boiling, reduce the heat to medium, then grab a spoon and swirl the water in a circle to create a little whirlpool. Slide your egg into the centre of the whirlpool by tipping the cup close to the water, then cook it for 3–4 minutes for a soft yolk. Remove the poached egg from the water with a spoon and repeat with the remaining egg.

Place the eggs on the salad and season. To serve, add a tablespoon of almond butter, a sprinkle each of pumpkin seeds and sunflower seeds, a pinch of paprika and a lemon wedge. Then take a snap for social media, because you'll be so proud of how amazing this looks!

Serves 2

TIPS
To speed things up, you can prepare the roasted sweet spud and hummus a day or two earlier. (Roasted sweet potato will keep in the fridge in a sealed container for 4–5 days, and so will the hummus.) Also, I just love the runny yolks in this recipe, but you can cook your eggs any way you like — unpeeled hard-boiled eggs will keep in the fridge for up to a week if you want to make this salad even easier.

This salad is bright, fresh and jam-packed with vitality. It makes a great side for just about any barbecued or grilled meat, but it's also satisfying as a main (another vegan beauty!). I love sunflower sprouts, but you can try broccoli sprouts, alfalfa or mung bean sprouts – they all look really sweet. And if you want to take the Mexicana theme to the next level, chop everything finely, grab a few corn chips and use them like little scoops.

mexicana avo SALAD

- 2 avocados, diced
- 1 x 400 g tin black beans, drained and rinsed
- 1 punnet (200 g) cherry tomatoes, halved
- 1 red capsicum, diced
- kernels of 1 fresh corn cob (I eat it raw but you can cook the corn if you prefer)
- 1 red onion, finely diced
- 1 cucumber, diced
- 1 bunch of coriander, leaves picked and chopped
- juice and zest of 1 lime
- 2 tablespoons extra-virgin olive oil
- 1 teaspoon cumin seeds, toasted
- salt flakes and freshly ground black pepper
- fresh sprouts (any kind), to serve

This recipe is a walk in the park. Seriously! Just pop everything into a large bowl, mix it all up and top with the sprouts.

Serves 4-6

I wanted to create something special to remind me of the amazing food I had with my best bud Linda at a Japanese-inspired health retreat we visited. Every meal was a work of art! But then I realised that this kind of fussiness just isn't me, so I came up with this salad instead. Don't be fooled – this light but nutrient-rich meal is surprisingly filling. The addition of dulse flakes – a delicious edible seaweed – gives you an extra antioxidant hit.

seaweed SALAD

- 1 head of butter lettuce, leaves washed, dried and shredded
- 1 carrot, grated or very finely sliced
- 1 beetroot, scrubbed and grated or very finely sliced
- 1 bunch of baby radishes, grated or very finely sliced
- 1 cup mung bean sprouts
- ¼ cup goji berries
- 1 tablespoon apple cider vinegar
- 2 tablespoons extra-virgin olive oil
- salt flakes and freshly ground black pepper
- 1 nori sheet, finely sliced
- ½ teaspoon dulse flakes
- 1 tablespoon sesame seeds, toasted

Combine the lettuce, carrot, beetroot, radish, sprouts and goji berries in a serving bowl and toss gently.

In a small jar or bowl, stir together the vinegar and olive oil and season to taste. Pour over the salad and toss lightly. Then simply top with the nori and dulse flakes and sprinkle over the toasted sesame seeds.

Serves 2

> **TIP**
> Dried seaweed softens as soon as it hits moisture, so I like to tuck in straight away while it's still crisp.

This is one of my favourite go-to meals when I'm having people over to dinner. I know I can whip it up in no time and be certain that they'll like it (as long as they eat fish). The citrus and mint combination is amazing, plus nutritionally it's the bee's knees.

crispy salmon with grapefruit and avo salad

- 1 pink grapefruit, peeled and segmented
- 1 avocado, diced
- 2 cups sunflower sprouts (or watercress, broccoli sprouts or snow pea sprouts)
- ½ bunch of mint, leaves picked
- 3 tablespoons extra-virgin olive oil
- 1 tablespoon sunflower seeds or pumpkin seeds
- 2 x 150–180 g salmon steaks, skin on
- salt flakes and freshly ground black pepper

To make the salad, combine the grapefruit, avocado, sprouts, mint and 1 tablespoon of the olive oil in a bowl and toss gently. Arrange on serving plates and sprinkle over the sunflower or pumpkin seeds.

Heat the remaining oil in a large frying pan over a medium–high heat. Place both of the salmon steaks in the pan skin-side down, and cook for about 3 minutes, or until the skin is crispy. Flip and cook the other sides for 1 minute if you like your salmon a little rare, or for 2 minutes if you prefer it cooked. To serve, pop the fish on top of the salad and season with salt and pepper. Tuck in!

Serves 2

Although this is a side dish, it looks so awesome in the centre of the dinner table I can guarantee it will steal the show! I love using micro coriander and purple radish sprouts to garnish this dish, but any fresh herb will do.

whole roasted CAULIFLOWER with almond butter sauce

1 head of cauliflower
4 tablespoons extra-virgin olive oil
salt flakes and freshly ground black pepper
¼ cup almond butter
juice of ½ lemon
½ cup almonds, activated if possible (see page 10), to serve
handful of fresh herbs, to serve

Preheat the oven to 200°C. Line two baking trays with baking paper.

Remove the rough outer leaves of the cauliflower, keeping a few of the smaller leaves intact, then cut the cauli into quarters.

Steam the cauliflower for 10 minutes in a large double-boiler or a saucepan with a steamer insert. Transfer the steamed cauli to the prepared baking trays (two quarters on each tray). Drizzle 1 tablespoon of olive oil over the cauliflower on each tray and season with salt and pepper. Bake for 15 minutes or until the tops are golden. (If the tops look a tad burnt, don't freak out – it'll add flavour!)

Meanwhile, place the almond butter, remaining olive oil and lemon juice in a food processor and blitz until creamy.

Now grab the almonds, pop them in a frying pan and toast them over a low heat for about 5 minutes, stirring often, or until they start to give off a lovely nutty aroma.

Remove the cauliflower from the oven and transfer to a serving platter. Spoon over the almond butter and sprinkle over the freshly toasted almonds. Scatter over the fresh herbs and serve immediately.

Serves 4

Soups are the ultimate 'fast' food. You can make them in big batches for the freezer, then grab them for lunches at work or easy dinners if you get home too knackered to cook. If you can't find rainbow chard (it's a type of silverbeet with bright red, yellow, pink or purple stalks), use ordinary silverbeet, spinach, kale or Tuscan cabbage.

chunky health nerd SOUP

- 2 tablespoons extra-virgin olive oil, plus extra to serve
- 1 onion, diced
- 1 leek, trimmed, washed thoroughly and sliced
- 2 garlic cloves, crushed or finely chopped
- 4 celery stalks, sliced
- 4 thyme sprigs, leaves picked
- 1.5 litres chicken stock
- 1 bunch of rainbow chard (or any dark leafy green – see above), stalks removed, leaves roughly chopped
- ½ green cabbage, cored and roughly chopped
- 2 carrots, sliced
- 1 sweet potato, cut into 2 cm chunks
- 3 handfuls of baby spinach leaves
- 1 x 400 g can chickpeas, drained and rinsed
- salt flakes and freshly ground black pepper
- 1 cup quinoa (any colour; I use a mix), rinsed
- 50 g piece of parmesan rind (optional)

To serve

- ½ bunch of coriander, leaves picked and chopped
- ½ cup chopped walnuts, activated if possible (see page 10)

Heat the olive oil in a large stockpot over a medium heat. Add the onion, leek, garlic and celery and sauté for 2–3 minutes, tossing them about a bit, until they begin to soften. Add the thyme, stock and remaining ingredients and bring to the boil. Reduce the heat to low, add the parmesan rind (if using) and simmer for about 20–25 minutes, or until the carrot and sweet potato are soft and the quinoa is cooked.

Serve topped with fresh coriander, chopped walnuts and a drizzle of olive oil.

Serves 6

Emma Christian and Emma Warren are two pretty special souls who make a lot of magic happen on a shoot. They are absolute whiz-kids in the kitchen, making sure the recipes are perfect and that they're looking spot-on for the photos. Even though I test and retest all my recipes, these girls don't let a single element slip. But the best bit is they have me in fits of laughter every day we work together. And that's what I think work should be – it's passionate, it's fun, it's hard work and stressful at times, but by god it's worth it. And if you can have a giggle along the way then I think you're set.

P.S. This salad is unreal. As soon as they made it and we'd shot it, I gobbled most of it up. It just feels so clean and fresh when you eat it. A winner in my books!

emmami SALAD

- 300 g salmon fillet, skin removed, cut into 1 cm dice
- 4 cups purple kale leaves, blanched, refreshed and water squeezed out
- 1 granny smith apple, cut into batons
- 4–6 radishes, cut into small wedges
- 1 tablespoon black sesame seeds
- bonito flakes, to serve
- purple radish sprouts (optional), to serve

Miso dressing
- 3 cm piece of ginger
- 2 tablespoons white miso paste
- 1/3 cup macadamia oil
- 1/2 teaspoon fish sauce
- juice of 1/2 lime

Salmon marinade
- 2 tablespoons mirin
- 2 tablespoons light soy sauce
- 2 teaspoons sesame oil
- juice of 1/2 lime

To make the miso dressing, finely grate the ginger and squeeze out the juice until you have 1 tablespoon of juice. Combine the ginger juice with the remaining dressing ingredients.

Combine the ingredients for the salmon marinade in a bowl. Add the diced salmon to the marinade and mix well with a spoon to coat. Leave to sit for at least 10 minutes to cure the salmon, then remove the salmon and discard the marinade.

Place the kale leaves on a large platter and drizzle with about three-quarters of the miso dressing. Scatter the salmon, apple and radish over the top. Drizzle over the remaining miso dressing then scatter with sesame seeds, bonito flakes and purple radish sprouts (if using) to serve.

Serves 2 as a main or 4–6 as a starter

TIPS
For an equally delicious version, use 2 cups of baby spinach leaves in place of the kale. You can leave the skin on the pumpkin, too, if you like.

I tried a delicious millet risotto for the first time when I visited the Aro Hā retreat in Queenstown, New Zealand. This is my slightly chunkier and more rustic version. It really hits the spot, especially on a chilly winter's night.

pumpkin and millet RISOTTO

1 butternut pumpkin, cut into 2 cm chunks (about 3 cups pumpkin pieces)

2 garlic cloves, grated

pinch each of salt flakes and freshly ground black pepper

3 tablespoons extra-virgin olive oil

1.25 litres vegetable or chicken stock

1 onion, diced

1 cup millet

1 bunch of kale, stalks removed, leaves finely chopped (about 3 cups of chopped kale)

1 tablespoon butter (or extra-virgin olive oil)

pumpkin seeds, to serve

Preheat the oven to 180°C. Line a baking tray with baking paper.

Place the pumpkin on the prepared tray. Sprinkle over the garlic and salt and pepper and drizzle over 2 tablespoons of the olive oil. Toss the pumpkin about a bit to coat in the seasoning. Bake for 20–30 minutes or until the pumpkin is golden brown.

Meanwhile, heat the stock in a covered saucepan over a medium heat until simmering. Reduce the heat and keep it at a low simmer while you cook the risotto.

Heat the remaining olive oil in a frying pan over a medium heat. Add the onion and sauté for 2–3 minutes, or until it starts to become translucent. Stir in the millet and 1 cup of the hot stock and bring to a simmer, stirring frequently. When the liquid is absorbed (the millet will start to look gluggy), add another ½ cup of hot stock (just like you would a regular risotto) and cook, stirring frequently, until it is all absorbed. Repeat this process with the remaining stock until the millet is soft and looks a bit like cooked quinoa (about 30–40 minutes). When the millet is tender, stir through the kale and let it wilt. Test the seasoning and add some salt and pepper if necessary. Add the roasted pumpkin and the butter or olive oil and heat through. Serve topped with the pumpkin seeds and enjoy!

Serves 4

This was my staple evening meal when I worked long hours at an organic grocery store. We were lucky enough to have access to a sweet little kitchen out the back, so I used to whip this up to keep us going.

moroccan nights VEGGIES

1 red onion, thinly sliced
1 zucchini, sliced into rounds
1 cup quartered brussels sprouts
1 cup chopped broccoli
1 sweet potato, scrubbed and chopped into chunks
2 tablespoons extra-virgin olive oil, plus extra to serve
2 garlic cloves, crushed
1 teaspoon ground cumin
1 teaspoon ground turmeric
½ teaspoon ground cinnamon
1 teaspoon paprika
¼ teaspoon cayenne pepper
pinch each of salt flakes and freshly ground black pepper

Preheat the oven to 180°C.

Place the chopped veggies on a baking tray or in a roasting tin. Drizzle over the olive oil then add the garlic, spices, salt and pepper. Now get in there with your hands and give everything a good old mix, making sure your veggies are covered with all the delicious flavours. Bake for 20–30 minutes, or until the veggies are soft and golden (check them with a fork).

Serve with an extra drizzle of olive oil.

Serves 2–4

TIPS
For a tasty variation, add 1 red capsicum chopped into large chunks, and some whole vine-ripened cherry tomatoes. Cauliflower chopped into large florets works really well too. Also, I've been known to whip this up in a rice cooker, though it definitely tastes best roasted in the oven.

Quinoa is all the rage at the moment because it's such a highly nutritious, gluten-free option to use in place of grains. I find white quinoa works well for any recipe, but I love to use the red and black varieties for savoury stuff (they have a stronger flavour and take a tad longer to cook). We've just started growing white quinoa here in Australia, which is awesome. Try to use homemade chicken stock if you can — it tastes so much better and is better for you!

mushroom, chicken and quinoa risotto

- ¼ cup extra-virgin olive oil
- 1 leek, trimmed, washed thoroughly and sliced
- 1 onion, sliced
- 2 garlic cloves, crushed
- 4 thyme sprigs, leaves picked
- 4–6 Swiss brown mushrooms, sliced
- 1½ cups white quinoa, rinsed
- 3 cups chicken stock
- salt flakes and freshly ground black pepper
- 4 chicken thighs, chopped into chunks

Heat 2 tablespoons of the olive oil in a large saucepan or stockpot over a medium heat. Add the leek, onion, garlic and thyme and sauté for 2 minutes. Add the mushrooms and cook for 5 minutes. Stir in the rinsed quinoa and the chicken stock and simmer, uncovered, for about 20 minutes, or until the quinoa is cooked (its little 'tails' will pop out and it will triple in size).

Meanwhile, heat the remaining olive oil in a frying pan over a medium heat. Season the chicken with salt (it helps it go crispier) and fry for 5–7 minutes, turning regularly, or until golden. Serve the quinoa and mushroom 'risotto' topped with the crispy chicken and finish with a good grind of black pepper.

Serves 4

TIPS
I've used chicken thighs in this recipe because they have heaps of flavour, but you can substitute two chicken breasts (organic if possible) if you like.

I also wipe (or brush) my mushrooms instead of washing them because they can get waterlogged and lose their flavour if you rinse them under water.

Gravlax is a traditional Scandinavian dish of salmon cold-cured in salt, sugar and dill. (It literally means 'buried salmon', from the medieval practice of preserving fish by burying it in the sand above the tide line.) This version is fun to make and perfect for a special occasion. A mate and I made it for Christmas one year and it was so tender and delicious. I mean, the colour alone is just so festive! If you want to make an alcohol-free version, use fresh orange juice instead of vodka. This recipe needs to be started 2 days in advance.

beetroot GRAVLAX with creamy mustard sauce

- 1 x 1 kg side of salmon, boned and skin removed (ask your fishmonger to do this)
- 1/3 cup raw sugar
- 1/3 cup coarse rock salt
- 3 beetroots, trimmed, peeled and grated
- 1 bunch of dill, roughly chopped (save a few sprigs for the top)
- 45 ml vodka

Creamy mustard sauce

- 1/2 cup ricotta
- 1 tablespoon wholegrain mustard
- 2 tablespoons extra-virgin olive oil
- zest and juice of 1 lemon
- salt flakes and freshly ground black pepper

Rinse the salmon and pat dry with paper towel. Place it in a dish or tray large enough to fit the whole side. Sprinkle over the sugar and rock salt, turning the fish to make sure it is evenly covered, then cover it with the grated beetroot and dill. Finally, drizzle over the vodka. Cover the dish with plastic wrap and place something weighty on top, such as a heavy chopping board or another dish filled with rocks. Refrigerate for 48 hours. When ready to serve, remove the salmon from the dish, scrape off the dill and beetroot and discard the marinating juices. Pat the salmon dry and slice it thinly using a sharp knife. Set aside to come to room temperature (10–15 minutes).

To make the creamy mustard sauce, combine the ricotta, mustard, olive oil and lemon juice in a blender jug and process until creamy. Season to taste.

Serve the salmon with a drizzle of mustard sauce, a sprig of dill and a pinch of lemon zest. Store any leftover salmon, covered, in the fridge for up to 3 days. The mustard sauce will keep in a sealed glass jar for 4–5 days.

Serves 6–8

I love this dish because it ticks all the clean green boxes and gives me a brilliant, fresh feeling that seems to last well into the next day. This recipe works well with most fish; I've made equally delicious versions with salmon, snapper and flathead.

barramundi with summery SALAD

- 1/3 cup extra-virgin olive oil
- 2 x 150 g barramundi fillets
- 2 big handfuls of rocket
- 2 big handfuls of baby spinach leaves
- 1 avocado, cut into chunks
- 1 punnet (250 g) strawberries, hulled and quartered
- 1/4 cup roughly chopped macadamia nuts, activated if possible (see page 10)
- 1/4 cup pumpkin seeds, plus extra to serve
- 1 tablespoon lemon juice
- salt flakes and freshly ground black pepper

Heat 2 tablespoons of the oil in a frying pan over a medium heat. Place the barramundi fillets in the pan skin-side down and press firmly with the back of a spatula to get an even, crispy skin. Fry for 3–4 minutes, then flip over and cook for 2–3 minutes on the other side. You'll know the fish is cooked when the flesh flakes easily with a fork.

Pop the rocket and spinach in a large serving bowl. Add the avocado, strawberries, macadamias and pumpkin seeds and toss gently. Dress with the remaining olive oil and the lemon juice and season to taste.

To serve, either flake the barramundi over the salad, or serve it whole with the salad on the side. Finish with an extra sprinkle of pumpkin seeds.

Serves 2

I know that sweet potato mashed with kale might sound a bit weird, but bear with me on this – it tastes amazing. This mash also works brilliantly with regular spuds, but I prefer to use sweet potato for the extra fibre, vitamin A and vitamin C.

porterhouse with kale and sweet spud mash

- 2 x 180 g porterhouse steaks
- 2 sweet potatoes, scrubbed and chopped into chunks
- ½ teaspoon cayenne pepper
- 1 red chilli, finely chopped (or 1 teaspoon chilli flakes) (optional)
- 1 big bunch of kale, stalks removed, leaves roughly chopped (5 packed cups of chopped kale leaves)
- 2 tablespoons extra-virgin olive oil
- salt flakes and freshly ground black pepper
- 1 garlic clove, smashed with the back of a knife
- 2 thyme sprigs
- 2 knobs of butter

Take the steaks out of the fridge and allow them to come to room temperature for about 20 minutes.

Meanwhile, pop the sweet spuds, cayenne pepper and chilli, if using, in a saucepan of water and bring to the boil over a medium–high heat. Reduce the heat and simmer for 10–15 minutes or until the potatoes are soft, adding the kale in the last 2 minutes. Remove from the heat, drain, then add 1 tablespoon of olive oil to the pan and season to taste. Mash the potatoes and kale together until you get the texture you like. Put a lid on the pan and keep warm.

Season the steaks with salt and pepper on both sides. Heat the remaining olive oil in a frying pan over a medium–high heat. Add the smashed garlic clove and thyme sprigs and give them a stir to flavour the oil. Pop the steaks in the pan and cook for 2–3 minutes on each side for medium–rare or 4–5 minutes for medium. I like to flip my steaks after every minute, but feel free to cook yours however you like. Add a knob of butter to each steak in the final minute of cooking, then remove from the heat and set aside to rest for at least 5 minutes. (The steaks will stay warm for 10 minutes, so don't be afraid to rest them.)

To serve, scoop some kale mash onto a warmed plate and pop the steak on top so the juices run into the veggies. Delish!

Serves 2

At the most basic level, our bodies need food, water, sleep and shelter. These are the big ones, and without them we'd die. Surviving, though, is way different from thriving. To flourish, our bodies need wholefoods, lots of hydration and restful sleep. We also need plenty of exercise. This doesn't mean you need to train like an ironman competitor, just find a form of movement that works for you. Plus, as we saw in the Mind chapter (page 53), paying attention to our mindset and emotions plays a huge role in our physical wellbeing.

BODY

> Keeping your body healthy is an expression of gratitude to the whole cosmos – the trees, the clouds, everything.
>
> Thích Nhất Hạnh, Buddhist monk, author and peace activist

EXERCISE

I love to exercise for the simple reason that it makes me feel good, which also happens to have the cool side effect of helping me to stick to a healthy eating plan. The theory goes that exercise (not the kind where you take a stroll to a cafe, but the full-bore kind where you're puffing and sweating) triggers the release of endorphins in the brain (natural chemicals that act like painkillers) and also boosts norepinephrine, a neurotransmitter that plays a role in mood. Some people think that exercise is the key to weight loss. It isn't. Yes, it can help you maintain a healthy weight, but only if you are also eating real food and minimising your intake of sugars, starches and processed carbs.

How you choose to exercise depends on your health goals. If your goal is to assist weight loss, then I would suggest a combo of cardio (running, boxing, power walking, bike-riding, swimming, skipping, dancing or anything that ramps your heart rate) and strength training (weights, CrossFit) at least twice a week. My trainer, Dan, does a combo of cardio and strength work with me, and I love it.

If your goal is to tone up, then strength work would be fine, and you can just do that at the gym any time you choose. If you want to improve your flexibility and feel emotionally calm and centred, you might choose yoga. My health goal is to be healthy and natural, so I do a little bit of cardio and strength training, but I also love walking and jogging in nature, and yoga is something I keep up most days because it just makes me feel good in my own skin. And for me that's what it's all about. I do what makes me feel my best but also what makes me happy. If you're not enjoying your workout, chances are you won't keep it up. Loving it and having fun with your training is key!

Best time of the day to exercise

It varies for everyone. I love to do cardio first thing in the morning on an empty tummy (at this time your body has fasted from the night before, so there's nothing new to burn off). Other people swear by a good sweat session after work to help them release any tension they've built up during the day. It's about trying different times and deciding what works best for you.

Foods for cardio training

Complete protein after any kind of exercise is the perfect fuel for the body. That said, if you're doing a lot of running, CrossFit or anything that gets your heart working at 80 per cent of its max, then you will need to up your carbs to refuel. Our body's primary energy source is from carbohydrates, and they are actually found in most foods, including grains, milk, fruit, vegetables, nuts and seeds. There are two types of carbs: simple carbs, including glucose, fructose and lactose; and complex carbs, found in nuts, seeds, legumes, whole grains and veggies (especially in root veggies like potatoes and sweet potatoes). Complex carbohydrates are the 'good' carbs because they slowly release energy in the body without creating an insulin spike (see Coming off Sugar, page 16) and your moods and energy levels will stay nice and even.

Note that because I follow paleo-inspired principles (and am gluten intolerant), I'm not into wheat, rye or other gluten-containing grains. I generally get my carbs from quinoa, banana, sweet spuds, millet, buckwheat and teff (another gluten-free ancient grain that looks a bit like poppy seeds and is high in protein, iron and fibre). But if you are okay with grains, please remember that refined, highly processed grains (the ones you find in bread, pasta, cereals, etc.) have had the outer husk and germ removed – the bits with all the nutritional benefits – and have a similar effect on the body as sugar. So think whole grains for more health benefits and slow-release energy.

Foods for strength training

If you're doing lots of strength work (I'm talking weights), then you'll need more protein to help repair and grow muscles. Think eggs, fish, meat and chicken. For energy, go for things like oats, bananas, sweet potato, brown rice, millet, amaranth and quinoa.

Foods for weight loss

The simplest way to lose weight is to eat high-protein, low-carbohydrate meals. The body has to work harder to digest and metabolise protein, so when you eat fewer carbs, there's less glucose around and the body has to burn fat to make ketones for energy – a metabolic process known as ketogenesis. Now this doesn't mean no carbs, just fewer carbs, so you still need to have oats, quinoa or paleo bread for brekkie, but stick to protein and veggies for lunches and dinners.

Note that I do not recommend eating this way in the long term as it's neither sustainable for the planet nor healthy for your body. If you eat an extremely high-protein diet with only a few carbs for a long time, it places great pressure on the kidneys to flush out all the excess ketones that are floating around. I prefer a balanced approach to eating: some carbs, some protein, some fats. If you are wanting to lose a lot of weight, it would be best to work with a healthcare professional.

Foods for maintaining a healthy weight

I'm all about healthy and natural, so I love a nutrient-dense smoothie for breakfast; a piece of fruit with a handful of nuts and seeds for a midmorning snack (bananas and macadamias are my favourite); a delishimo salad for lunch with protein (say an egg or leftover meat) and complex carbs (like sweet potato, quinoa or buckwheat); a little bit of raw chocolate for my arvo snack; then a simple protein-plus-veggies meal at night (my fave is crispy salmon with kale and broccoli, though sometimes I'll add sweet potato if I know I'm exercising the next morning).

YOGA

Yoga is the gift I give to myself and to others (when I teach). The practice of yoga, for me, is less about the physical benefits (flexibility and 'yoga abs') and much more about the emotional clarity and calmness it gives me. I feel more connected, more open in my heart and happier.

The word yoga literally means 'to be in union' (yoke) with your higher self, allowing you to be the best version of you. I love learning what Sanskrit words mean, like *sakshin*, which means 'the witness', the quiet observer beneath the constant chatter of our everyday consciousness, or *chitta*. Then there's *sukha*, meaning bliss and happiness, that magical state of balance between strength and softness.

Heaps of people don't try yoga because they think they have to be flexible to be able to do it. Not so! I'm pretty inflexible for a yogi, but I just work hard at it and practise lots. One of the main reasons for practising yoga 'asana' (the physical poses) is to calm the unruly mind. In fact, it is said that the real yoga starts at the end of the class when you leave the mat and take your calm mind with you.

Choosing a style

It's amazing how many different styles of yoga there are: hatha, ashtanga, vinyasa, Bikram, Iyengar, kundalini . . . the list goes on and on. I've actually tried quite a few of them and they are all wonderful. If you're a beginner, just ask at the studio and they can help you choose the right class.

Yin

I practise and teach yin. In this style, poses are held for a long time (5–7 minutes), which requires you to really focus your attention. It's a slow, meditative style, where the poses work more on tendons and fasciae than muscles. (See page 183 for more on yin yoga.)

Vinyasa

I also practise and teach vinyasa, where movement is linked to your breathing to create a continuous, dynamic flow. I love how each asana flows into the next with every breath, opening up your heart and mind – it's very empowering and inspiring.

Bikram

Loads of people start out with Bikram yoga (I did). It's also called 'hot yoga' because the room is heated to about 40°C and the humidity is ramped up to 40–50 per cent. It's pretty full-on. The classes take 90 minutes and there are 26 postures, most of which you do twice. The instructor says exactly the same thing at every class, which helps to discipline the mind. I still enjoy doing the occasional Bikram class, but I also love moving my body in other ways, which is why I practise other forms of yoga.

YOGA at home

I love how portable yoga is; you can even do it without a mat (though it is easier if you have one). All you need is a little bit of space. I do it in my hotel room when I travel. Here are some sequences and poses that you can try at home.

Basic warm-up

This is the basic warm-up that kicks off any vinyasa yoga class I teach. It gets you into a standing position to begin Salute to the sun A overleaf. It's all about getting into the zone with your breathing and warming up your spine. Step 1 (*balasana*) is used as part of the warm-up here, but it also doubles as a restorative pose (see page 129).

Step 1.

Start in child's pose (*balasana*). With your toes touching, slide your knees apart until your torso fits between your thighs. Rest your forehead on the mat. Stretch your fingertips forward and lengthen your spine. Take three deep breaths in and out through the nose, and feel the earth below you.

Step 2.

Now warm up your spine with the cat–cow stretch (*chakravakasana*). Start on all fours with a neutral (flat) spine.

Step 3.
Inhale and dip your spine, lifting your gaze as you do so. This is the cow stretch.

Step 4.
Exhale and arch your spine like an angry cat! Continue to inhale for cow and exhale for cat for 4–6 reps, then return to neutral spine.

TIP It's really fun to do yoga to music, so pop on your favourite tunes.

Step 5.
From neutral spine, move your hands forward by one handprint length, hook your toes under and straighten your legs into downward-facing dog (*adho mukha svanasana*). Draw your heels towards the ground, plant your palms down and roll your shoulders away from your ears. Take 5 deep breaths and then slowly walk your feet towards your hands and gradually roll up to standing. Now you're ready for Salute to the sun A!

TIP This is a resting pose, believe it or not. Think of it as your home base.

YOGA at home

Salute to the sun A

This sequence is a great way to warm the body up in the morning. Once you get used to the poses and create more flow between them you will build *tapas* (heat) in the body, both physically and spiritually. Repeat this sequence at least three times.

Step 1.

Stand in mountain pose (*tadasana*) with your feet shoulder-width apart, your shoulders back and your palms outstretched. (Imagine yourself sayin 'ta-da!')

TIP This is the pose to set an intention for your class or home sequence. That could be self-love, to be happy or to be healthy.

Step 2.

Inhale, look up and bring your arms up above your head, with your palms facing each other.

Step 3.

Exhale and move into a forward fold (*uttanasana*). Some people can bring their heads quite close to their knees, but just gently lengthen your back and leg muscles as far as you can (it's fine to bend your knees). In my first forward fold, I like to take a few breaths and shake my head to loosen my neck.

Step 4.

Move into a halfway lift by bringing your fingertips to the floor or your shins, with your shoulders back.

Step 5.

Inhale, bend your knees, place your hands flat on the floor and then jump or step back into a high plank. Stack your shoulders over your wrists, turn your core on and think about sucking your navel to your spine.

Step 6.

Exhale and lower your arms into a low plank or *chaturanga dandasana*. Hug your elbows in, keep your core strong and shift your weight forward. This pose will feel challenging – it really fires up the core!

continued overleaf

YOGA at home

Salute to the sun A

Step 7.
Inhale, then roll your toes forward so that you are resting on the tops of your feet. Keep your hips close to the ground, your elbows close to your ribs and stretch your torso into cobra pose (*bhujangasana*).

TIP Back bends like this open your heart and lift your mood.

Step 7a.
When you reach this point in your second rep, you have the option to move into an upward-facing dog (*urdhva mukha svanasana*) rather than cobra if you can, as your spine will be nice and warm. (Do the same for your third rep.) Lift your gaze and make sure your thighs are off the mat.

Step 8.
Exhale, roll over your toes, push your hands into the mat and use your core to lift yourself into downward-facing dog (*adho mukha svanasana*). Remember, you can always take a few breaths in down dog.

Step 9.
Inhale and exhale then, on the 'no breath', jump or step forward with both feet. You are now back in *uttanasana* (step 3).

Step 10.
Inhale and reach up with outstretched arms (see step 2).

Step 11.
Exhale and lower your arms into *tadasana* (step 1). Then repeat steps 2–11 again for three sets in total.

Now that you've warmed up, you could move into what I like to call the 'sun Bs', with a few warrior poses, arm balances and back bends, before slowing it down with some hip-openers. You'll find these poses overleaf.

my favourite YOGA POSES

Here is a collection of personal favourites that you can incorporate into your home routine following your Salute to the sun A warm-up. Most of these are intermediate or advanced poses, so only try them at home once you've mastered them in a class with a qualified instructor.

Heart-opener poses

These poses help to open the chest and heart space and can help to release negative energy.

1. Camel pose (ustrasana)

A truly heart-opening back bend! I do this pose before leaving the house whenever I go on a date to keep my heart super open. You'll want to be warmed up for this pose. Keep your core and glutes turned on to protect your spine. Hips forward, chest up.

2. Wild thing (camatkarasana)

This pose is also called flash dance and is so much fun to do. It's not too hard, and feels great to stretch and open. Think about lifting your heart skyward.

3. Dancer's pose
(*natarajasana*)

This is my absolute favourite for balance and heart opening. Think about kicking up and back, and keeping the heart open.
My tip? Enjoy falling out and always get back up again.

4. Wheel pose
(*urdhva dhanurasana*)

This is a brilliant heart opener and a great pose to stimulate energy in the body. I'd recommend starting with a bridge pose (*setu bandha sarvangasana*) before trying this more advanced back bend. Think about lifting your heart back past your hands.

Hip-opener poses

Opening the hips can help to ease back pain and stiffness, and increase mobility. Tight hips are often the result of too much time at the desk, so these poses are really useful for most of us.

1. Sleeping butterfly
(*supta badha konasana*)

This is a key pose in yoga and a great one to start off your practice. If you don't have a bolster, simply roll up a blanket instead. Place at the base of the spine (don't sit on it) so that it supports your lower back and all the way up to your head. Pop the soles of your feet together, let them peel open like a book and feel your hips to open out. If that feels super uncomfortable (and it might for a while), place a pillow under each knee.

continued overleaf

my favourite YOGA POSES

Hip-opener poses

2. Sleeping swan (eka pada rajakapotasana)

Also known as half-pigeon, this yin pose can be a little uncomfortable at first. Try lying on a bolster or putting a block under your hip.

TIP We hold current issues in our hips, so if you can, leave them here on the mat. This pose is also a restorative one (see opposite).

Arm balances

Not only do these poses help build strength in your arms and core muscles, they are great for focusing the mind.

1. Crow (bakasana)

This one is easier than it looks. It's all about keeping your abs turned on and your gaze forward. Your arms essentially become a shelf for your knees.

2. Baby crow (baby bakasana)

Another sweet arm balance. Tuck your knees in as close to your armpits as you can and then balance with your nose almost touching the ground.

Restorative poses

When you are learning new poses it can be helpful to rest every now and again, especially if you are doing some of the stronger standing poses.

1. Legs-up-the-wall (*viparita karani*)

This is part of my pre-bed ritual. Simply lie on your back and put your legs straight up the wall for at least 3 minutes (or as long as 15). It's that simple.

This pose is a passive, supported version of a shoulder stand and has a calming effect on the nervous system. It has even been used to help treat depression.

2. Pose of the child (*balasana*)

This is the perfect chill-out pose to come back to at any point during a yoga class or sequence if you need a break. See the warm-up for Salute to the sun A on page 120 for a detailed description.

3. Twisted roots

This is another yin pose. I like to do this one for 3–5 minutes on each side before bed – it's super calming and restorative.

TIP My yin teacher, Hugh, told me that we hold past issues in our spines and to try and leave them on the yoga mat.

4. Corpse pose (*savasana*)

At the end of every yoga practice, no matter how long it is, take the time to rest in *savasana* for 5 minutes. Simply lie on your back with your arms by your sides (not touching your body) and your palms facing upward. Cover yourself with a blanket. Close your eyes.

Take a big breath in through the nose then relax as you exhale through the mouth. At first the stillness can feel strange, but the more you do it the more you realise how amazing and powerful it is to simply lie still. If you find it hard to keep still (sometimes I do) it can be nice to have a *savasana* song – just make sure it's super calming.

SLEEP

Most of us totally underestimate the importance of sleep. We're so busy doing a million and one things that we just soldier on, telling ourselves we'll be fine and we can catch up tomorrow night. But our bodies need sleep to rest and repair, and if we don't get enough of it we can't concentrate, our short-term memory is affected, and we're physically clumsy and have poor reaction times. The other huge problem with not getting enough sleep is that it messes with our appetite hormones. I know that as soon as I have a few nights with less sleep, I'm much hungrier than usual and I start craving sweet things.

I always advise clients who are beginning a new, healthier eating plan to go to bed early before their first day. This helps to keep their minds clear and focused for the whole day. (Our willpower is usually stronger in the morning than it is in the evening, so if you've had a good sleep you're giving yourself a better chance of staying on track.)

Tips for a good night's sleep

Avoid stimulants
Coffee, chocolate, caffeinated tea and even chillies last thing at night rev up your metabolism so it's harder to achieve that relaxed state you need to drift off to sleep. If you love your caffeine, stick to just one coffee or tea at the beginning of the day.

Make a task list for tomorrow
If you're someone who likes to be organised, get this stuff out of your head and onto paper (or into your phone) as it helps to put your mind at ease. It feels like you've made a start, so you don't need to go over and over things in your head.

Have a bed-time ritual
Studies show that the brain learns to switch into rest mode if you perform the same little rituals every night. Try popping on some chilled music (I love the mellow stuff on rainymood.com), lighting a candle, reading a book or having some herbal tea – whatever works for you. (See page 227 for some calming night-time teas.) I love to put on my Himalayan salt lamp and fairy lights (yes, I have fairy lights in my bedroom) and sprinkle a few drops of lavender oil on my pillow.

Keep technology out of your bedroom
This can be a hard one, but it means you'll sleep better. My laptop doesn't come into the bedroom unless I'm watching a movie on it. I don't have a TV, and I don't look at my phone for 20 minutes before I sleep. I set my alarm on my phone, pop it on silent, then keep it on the other side of the room, face down.

Try some gentle yoga
There are lots of gentle, relaxing yoga poses you can do. See the restorative poses on page 129.

DETOXING your life

I'm a big believer in minimising the toxins that we invite into our bodies every day, whether we ingest them from our foods, apply them to our skin and hair, or breathe them in from the clothes we wear, the furniture we touch and the environment around us. Have a look at the chemicals you're using around your home. Do you use insecticides, fungicides or weedicide in your house or garden, or do you use natural alternatives? What about paints and solvents and glues? Then there are the cleaning products you use in your kitchen, bathroom and laundry, and even the plastics you use for storing food.

Skin and hair products

The skin is the body's largest organ and soaks up 60–90 per cent of anything you put on it, so try to use products with ingredients that are as close to nature as possible. Unfortunately, this is easier said than done. Heaps of products are labelled 'natural' and 'organic', but you'll need to do your research as there's a big difference between what cosmetic companies call 'organic' and what food producers are permitted to label as 'certified organic'. Organic in non-food products simply means carbon-based, so by this definition petroleum jelly or even petrol can be classed as organic as they contain carbon!

Parabens are a particularly dodgy ingredient in cosmetics and hair products. They're made from petrochemicals and are used as preservatives (e.g. methylparaben, butylparaben and propylparaben) and, like plastics, are hormone disruptors. Studies show that they can mimic oestrogen (which can mess with hormones) and they've also been detected in human breast cancer tissues. In addition, some researchers have found that methylparaben applied to the skin reacts with UVB (the sun's ultraviolet B shortwave rays) and may lead to rapid skin ageing and DNA damage.

While parabens occur naturally at low levels in certain foods, they are metabolised when eaten, which reduces their oestrogenic effect. The parabens in cosmetics, however, are absorbed directly into the body through the skin.

My advice would be to read the label, talk to your mates about what they use and do some research about all of the ingredients. In a dream world the list should almost read like a list of wholefoods. In fact, why not try to make your own masks and moisturisers? I do! That way I can make them fresh and I get to add that extra secret ingredient that makes the world of difference: love.

Foodie facial

This face mask leaves your skin feeling lush and glowing. The avocado supplies the good fats, the raw honey has antibacterial qualities, and the cacao is high in antioxidants.

1 mashed avocado
1 tablespoon cacao powder
1 tablespoon raw honey
1 tablespoon melted coconut oil

Mix all the ingredients well in a cup and then spread gently over your face. Lie back and let it do its magic for 10 minutes. Rinse off with warm water and gently pat dry.

Tip: You won't be looking your best with this all over your moosh, so maybe don't answer the door!

Easiest night treatment ever

If you're prone to dry skin, take a small dab of cold-pressed extra-virgin coconut oil and apply it gently to the skin on your face and neck.

I leave mine on all night but you don't have to, especially if you have a combination of dry and oily skin – in which case you could rinse it off with warm water after 10–20 minutes. Do this three times a week and you'll notice a new softness and glow!

To help prevent fine lines around the eyes, I use a drop of organic rosehip oil at night. I pop it on right before bed.

Super-natural hair treatment

Massage 1 tablespoon of good-quality extra-virgin olive oil through the ends of your hair (avoid the roots unless you want the greasy look).

Take your shampoo and pop it on your scalp before you wet your hair. (If you try to wet your oiled hair first, it just runs off and the shampoo has nothing to lather with.) Now jump in the shower, rinse and condition.

The real secret to glowing skin and hair

Do you want to know the secret to glowing skin and hair?

I'll give you a hint: it's got nothing to do with fancy creams and shampoos. It's what you eat – specifically, whether you eat enough good fats along with your protein and veggies. I'm talking plenty of polyunsaturated omega-3s (found in nuts, seeds and oily fish), a little bit of mono-unsaturated fat (avocados and extra-virgin olive oil), and a small amount of saturated fat (e.g. coconut oil and eggs). Loads of people are scared of coconut oil because it is so high in saturated fat, but it's a medium-chain saturated fat, which means the body will try to use it for energy first rather than store it. That said, if you do eat too much of it, it will be stored.

Cleaning products

I have a mate who couldn't get rid of skin rashes until he realised he was reacting to the chemicals in his laundry powder. And he only discovered this when the powder ran out and he got a different brand! Working out what is safe and what isn't is tricky in Australia, because cleaning-product manufacturers are not required to list the ingredients on the label. Even worse, we have no legislation covering the use of the word 'organic' for household products (though we do for food and food-grade products), so manufacturers can freely use the word 'green' and 'organic' on their labels no matter what the contents are.

A recent study in Melbourne found that several so-called 'green' products, especially those that were scented or fragranced, actually contained the same kinds of hazardous chemicals as the 'non-green' ones. A fragrance is a bunch of different chemicals, usually synthetic ones, that include terpenes, which are toxic in themselves but produce secondary pollutants when they react with ozone in the air.

The best thing to do is to steer clear of artificially scented products and do some research online. Look for a reputable brand of sustainable cleaning products (I like ecostore) or try making your own.

Homemade spray cleaner

Try this recipe to harness the cleaning power of white vinegar.

1 cup white vinegar
1 cup water

Mix in a spray bottle and use as you would any other surface cleaner. Add a few drops of eucalyptus oil or pure lavender oil if you like.

Homemade bathroom cleaner

This homemade scrub is great for cleaning tiles, bathtubs, sinks and even your toilet.

¾ cup bicarbonate of soda
¼ cup water

Mix the bicarb soda and water well to make a thick paste. Apply to the surface with a soft, clean cloth. Rinse. (Note that if your shower recess is acrylic, you might need to test the mixture on a little patch first in case it scratches.)

Plastics

There are two types of plastic that are considered potentially harmful to our health: polyvinyl chloride or PVC (used in plastic bottles, some plastic wraps, and the seals on screw-top jar lids) and polycarbonate (used to make food storage containers and bottles as well as the epoxy resin lining in tin cans).

PVC contains phthalates, and polycarbonate contains bisphenol A (BPA), both of which are endocrine disruptors, meaning they mimic hormones in the body. An increasing number of studies suggest a link between exposure to these chemicals and problems such as infertility, cancer, obesity, heart disease and diabetes. In Australia, most major retailers have voluntarily phased out polycarbonate plastic baby bottles containing BPA, but there's no actual legislation yet (as there is in the USA and EU).

You can often identify the type of plastic from its identification code — unfortunately, this code is also voluntary (!), so you won't find it on all plastic packaging. The number 3 in a little triangle usually means PVC, and number 7 is polycarbonate.

The other plastics are all okay: number 1 is polyethylene terephthalate (PET), used in water and soft-drink bottles; number 2 is high-density polyethylene (HDPE), used in milk containers and yoghurt cups; number 4 is low-density polyethylene (LDPE), used in takeaway containers; number 5 is polypropylene (PP); and number 6 is polystyrene (PS).

Avoid buying plastic-wrapped meat, fruit or vegetables from supermarkets, butchers and greengrocers as many are still using PVC plastic wrap. Also, avoid reusable plastic bottles with the symbol 7 (or look for product labels that say 'BPA-free'). Note that heating and washing polycarbonate bottles can increase the amount of BPA that leaches out.

While the plastics in takeaway containers are supposed to be safe, it's probably best to avoid using any plastic containers when cooking or reheating food in a microwave oven. I don't use a microwave, but if you do, use glass containers for high-fat foods, as toxic chemicals are more likely to migrate into fatty foods at high temperatures.

I love to use glass for all of my food and drink when I can; I know it's much heavier, but I reckon it's the healthiest. Aluminium drinking bottles are pretty popular, too, though some have a plastic lining, so either ask questions or choose stainless steel instead.

crystal POWER

I'm really passionate about crystals. I've even done crystal healing courses, which sounds a bit out there but is actually fascinating and beautiful. It is based on the folkloric belief that crystals and gemstones hold energy that can facilitate healing and growth. Here are a few of the most well-known crystals and their qualities. (These are just the tip of the iceberg!)

Amethyst
mental, physical and spiritual healing

Rose quartz
healing wounds related to the heart

Clear quartz
cleansing and also amplifying the healing powers of other crystals

Labradorite
making dreams come true

Peacock ore
starting anew

I have crystals in my room for good luck and to help me focus on my goals; I even sleep with a hunk of labradorite under my pillow every night to help me manifest my dreams. In many ways, crystals are like little affirmations that I can touch, reminding me that I feel positive about life.

Some say that crystals will find you, so if you stumble across a hippie crystal shop and a particular gem or crystal calls your name, take it home. Don't read up about it first or get the shopkeeper to explain – just trust your intuition and buy it.

It's no secret that I have a sweet tooth, which might seem a bit ironic given all that we know about sugar's role in obesity, diabetes and heart disease. But for me, living a healthy, happy life is not about depriving yourself of the things you love — it's about finding healthier alternatives. And while there *are* healthier alternatives to processed table sugar (such as maple syrup, rice malt syrup, honey and dates), it's important to remember that they are still treats and must be consumed in moderation. So even though they might contain more nutrients (e.g. honey) or create less of a blood sugar spike (e.g. rice malt syrup), your body still metabolises them in the same way. For that reason, I often go for sweeteners like stevia and monk fruit, which have the least impact on blood sugar levels. Just make sure you go for the pure forms, as lots of the versions you can buy in supermarkets have had other sugars added (check the label).

salted caramel and cinnamon MACADAMIAS

These are so amazingly delicious it's hard not to eat them all in one day! You'll love the sweet and spicy aroma.

- ²/₃ cup maple syrup
- ½ teaspoon ground cinnamon
- ½ teaspoon ground nutmeg
- ¼ teaspoon ground ginger
- pinch of salt flakes
- 4 cups macadamia nuts, activated if possible (see page 10)
- 1 tablespoon shredded (or desiccated) coconut
- 1 tablespoon filtered water

Line a baking tray with baking paper.

Heat the maple syrup, spices and salt in a large saucepan over a medium heat. When the mixture starts to bubble, add the nuts, coconut and filtered water. Cook, uncovered, for 5–7 minutes, or until the liquid evaporates, stirring continuously so the nuts are covered and the sugar doesn't burn.

Spread the nuts in an even layer on the prepared tray and leave to cool and harden (about 20 minutes). Then dive on them (that's what I usually do)! Store them in an airtight container in the pantry for up to 6 months.

Makes 4 cups

TIP
This recipe works really well with pecans and walnuts, too, but I reckon it would work with pretty much any nut. Try it with almonds, brazil nuts, hazelnuts, pistachios …

Warning: this is *very* addictive. When I first made it, it didn't last very long at all. Spread it on some paleo bread for brekkie, serve it with a muffin for a snack, or just do like I do and eat it by the teaspoonful!

maple macadamia NUT BUTTER

3 cups macadamia nuts, activated if possible (see page 10)

½ cup coconut oil, melted

½ cup maple syrup

pinch of ground cinnamon

tiny pinch of salt flakes

Pop your ingredients into a food processor and blitz until smooth (the more powerful your processor the less time it will take). Transfer to a jar, or jars, and store in the fridge for yonks.

Makes 3 cups

TIP
If you're not happy with the consistency, add a little more melted coconut oil.

flavoured coconut SUGARS

Here's a fun way to add a bit of pizzazz to your sweet treats. Simply use any of these in a recipe that calls for coconut sugar where you think the flavour combo might work. Remember, though, that even though coconut sugar is less refined and has a lower glycaemic index than white sugar (and is a great natural source of minerals and dietary fibre), it is still a sugar and as such needs to be used in moderation. If you prefer, you can use xylitol (if you can tolerate it: some people experience gas and bloating) or erythritol (a sugar alcohol). Each of these recipes makes 1 cup, but feel free to halve the quantities if you want to try a smaller batch first.

cinnamon coconut SUGAR

- 1 cup coconut sugar
- 2 tablespoons ground cinnamon

Place ingredients in an airtight container and shake to mix. Add to your morning porridge, to roasted pumpkin or sweet spuds, and to baked or poached fruit. Store in an airtight container in the pantry for 8–12 months.

lime coconut SUGAR

- 1 cup coconut sugar
- zest of 1 lime

Stir the lime zest through the coconut sugar and store in an airtight container in the fridge for 2 weeks. This is brilliant with cocktails, or sprinkled over coconut ice cream to make a coco-lime splice. I also love it on a slice of paleo bread spread with coconut oil. Delishimo!

ginger coconut SUGAR

1 cup coconut sugar
1 teaspoon ground ginger

Mix together and store in an airtight container in the pantry for 8–12 months. This one is yummy sprinkled on baked figs, granola, porridge or candied nuts.

pumpkin pie spice coconut SUGAR

1 cup coconut sugar
2 tablespoons ground cinnamon
½ teaspoon ground nutmeg
pinch of ground cloves

I love a pinch of this in my chia porridge or whatever energy ball mixture I'm making. Store in an airtight container in the pantry for 8–12 months.

vanilla coconut SUGAR

1 cup coconut sugar
1 vanilla pod (or ¾ teaspoon vanilla powder)

Place the sugar in an airtight container, then split and scrape out the vanilla seeds and stir them through. Place the pod casing in the container as well, to enhance the vanilla flavour. I love this creation sprinkled over quinoa porridge or fresh fruit. Store in an airtight container in the pantry for 8–12 months.

These guys taste a bit like the delicious sesame-based Middle Eastern treat halva, hence the name. Sesame seeds are full of mono-unsaturated fats, which are good for the brain. You can use any sweetener of your choice in place of the maple syrup.

HALVA brain balls

- 1 cup dried figs
- ½ cup almond meal
- 1 tablespoon coconut oil, melted
- ¼ cup almond butter
- ¼ cup tahini (hulled or unhulled)
- 2 tablespoons maple syrup
- ½ teaspoon ground cinnamon
- ¼ teaspoon ground nutmeg
- pinch of salt flakes
- ¾ cup sesame seeds, toasted, for rolling

Pop all of the ingredients except the sesame seeds in a food processor and process until well combined.

Place the sesame seeds in a small bowl. Roll the mixture into little balls and dip them in the sesame seeds to coat.

Store in the fridge in a sealed container for up to 2 weeks (or freeze for longer).

Makes 12–14

These little beauties are great to munch on after training, and if you choose to add protein powder (you don't have to) they'll really keep you going. They are my personal favourite! Rolling them is much easier with slightly damp hands. These also freeze really well.

LEMON and lime protein bites

- 1½ cups almond meal
- ½ cup desiccated coconut
- ½ cup coconut oil, melted
- 3 tablespoons maple syrup
- zest of 1 lemon
- juice of 2 lemons
- zest and juice of 1 lime
- 2 tablespoons vanilla protein powder (optional)
- seeds of 1 vanilla pod (or ½ teaspoon vanilla powder)
- pinch of salt flakes
- 1 cup shredded (or desiccated) coconut, plus extra for rolling

Place all of the ingredients except the extra coconut for rolling in a food processor. Blend until the mixture forms a very thick batter.

Place the shredded coconut in a bowl. Take heaped teaspoonfuls of the mixture and form them into little balls, then dip them in the coconut to evenly coat.

Pop them in the fridge for about 20 minutes to firm up and you've got the perfect tangy treat! Store them in the fridge in a sealed container for up to 2 weeks.

Makes about 20

I love cookies and I love carrot cake made with warming spices like cinnamon and nutmeg, so I thought, why not combine the two? These paleo cookies look super cute and make brilliant pressies! They freeze really well for up to 3 months.

carrot cake COOKIES

- 1 cup almond meal
- ¼ cup coconut flour
- 1 teaspoon gluten-free baking powder
- ½ teaspoon ground cinnamon
- ¼ teaspoon ground nutmeg
- seeds of 1 vanilla pod (or ½ teaspoon vanilla powder)
- pinch of salt flakes
- 1 cup coconut sugar (or sweetener of your choice)
- 1 cup almond butter
- 2 eggs, beaten
- 1 carrot, grated
- ½ cup sultanas

Preheat the oven to 180°C. Line a baking tray with baking paper.

Place all the dry ingredients in a big mixing bowl and give them a good stir. Add the almond butter, eggs, carrot and sultanas and mix well. Roll the cookie dough into balls and place them on the prepared tray. Press them lightly with the back of a fork.

Pop the tray in the fridge for 1 hour, then bake for 8–10 minutes or until the cookies are nice and golden. Then have one while they're still hot – they taste so-o-o good!

Makes 12

I love the comforting sweetness of pumpkin and almonds, especially when they're teamed with warming spices like cinnamon and nutmeg. These cookies are guaranteed to make you feel good, especially shared with some mates over a hot cuppa. If you don't want to use sultanas, use chocolate chips instead. These freeze really well.

pumpkin pie COOKIES

- ½ cup almond butter
- ¾ cup steamed, mashed pumpkin
- ½ cup almond meal
- ½ cup sultanas (optional)
- 2 cm piece of ginger, grated (or ½ teaspoon ground ginger)
- ½ teaspoon ground cinnamon, plus extra for sprinkling
- ¼ teaspoon ground cloves
- ¼ teaspoon ground nutmeg
- 1 tablespoon maple syrup
- seeds of 1 vanilla pod (or ½ teaspoon vanilla powder)
- pinch of salt flakes
- 1 tablespoon coconut sugar, for sprinkling (optional)

Preheat the oven to 180°C. Line one or two baking trays with baking paper.

Place all of the ingredients in a large bowl and stir until well combined. The mixture should be quite sticky. Place heaped teaspoonfuls of the mixture on the prepared tray or trays. Press them lightly with the back of a fork if you like (that's what my grandma always did), and give them a sprinkle of coconut sugar (if desired) plus an extra sprinkle of cinnamon.

Bake for 12–15 minutes, or until golden. Enjoy them warm or wait for them to cool down first (if you can!).

Makes 12

I feel really lucky to have my friend Karina in my life. She's real, honest and hardworking, not to mention amazing when it comes to food! This creation is hers. Thank you, KD, for inspiring me to be the best person I can be.

karina's pretty RASPBERRY and coconut slice

Base

10 medjool dates

1 cup shredded coconut

2 tablespoons raw cacao

2 tablespoons chia seeds

1 tablespoon almond butter

1 tablespoon coconut oil, melted

Topping

2 cups cashews, soaked for 2–3 hours (or overnight) then rinsed

¼ cup coconut oil, melted

1 teaspoon ground cinnamon

¼ cup coconut cream

juice of ½ lemon

1 heaped tablespoon raw honey

1 cup fresh or frozen raspberries

To serve

1 teaspoon freeze-dried raspberry powder

shredded coconut

edible gold leaf (optional)

1 cup fresh raspberries

Line an 18 x 28 cm slice tin with plastic wrap.

Place the base ingredients in a food processor and blend until combined and the mixture starts to stick together. Press evenly into the base of the lined tin and refrigerate while you make the topping.

To make the topping, place the soaked cashews, coconut oil, cinnamon, coconut cream, lemon juice and honey in a food processor and blend until very smooth and silky. Once the mixture is smooth, gently fold through the raspberries. Pour the mixture over the chilled base and smooth to create a flat surface. Sprinkle over the raspberry powder, shredded coconut and, if you are feeling extra special, some edible gold leaf.

Place in the freezer for 1 hour (or the fridge for 3 hours) to set completely. Sprinkle over the fresh raspberries, cut into squares and serve.

Makes 18–20 pieces

I know the idea of adding black beans to brownies might sound weird, but trust me, this recipe is an abolute beauty. My amazing friend Karina (yes, Karina again!) introduced me to bean brownies back when I was her nutritionist. She just turned up with a batch for me one day (she's thoughtful like that). Thanks for the inspiration, KD.

beanie BROWNIE

- 1 x 400 g can black beans, drained and rinsed (to reduce the phytic acid)
- 3 eggs
- 3 tablespoons coconut oil, melted
- 3 tablespoons cacao powder
- seeds of 1 vanilla pod (or ½ teaspoon vanilla powder)
- pinch of salt flakes
- ¾ cup maple syrup
- ⅓ cup roughly chopped walnuts, activated if possible (see page 10)
- coconut ice cream (optional), to serve

Preheat the oven to 180°C. Line the base and sides of an 18 x 18 cm brownie tin with baking paper.

Place all of the ingredients except the walnuts and ice cream in a food processor and whiz until smooth. Remove the processor's cover and blade, then stir the walnuts through the mixture. (This way they'll stay chunky, and will be like little nuggets of gold in the finished brownie). Using a spatula, scrape the mixture into the prepared tin, smoothing the top. Bake for 25–30 minutes, or until a skewer inserted into the middle comes out clean.

These are delicious warm or cold, but if you really want to take them to the next level, try them with a scoop of coconut ice cream.

Makes 9 pieces

TIP
If you're not keen on walnuts, try macadamias, pistachios or any nut you love.

mango, macadamia and lemon myrtle SLICE

When I lived on the Gold Coast, I loved going to the Byron Bay and Bangalow farmers' markets. I'd get so excited about the new ingredients I might discover! This slice reminds me of the macadamia nut butter I used to buy from one little old lady – it was much better than anything I've ever had, to this day.

- 1 cup almond meal
- 1 cup finely chopped macadamia nuts, activated if possible (see page 10)
- 1 mango, diced
- 3 eggs
- seeds of 1 vanilla pod (or ½ teaspoon vanilla powder)
- ¼ cup macadamia oil
- ½ teaspoon ground lemon myrtle leaf

Preheat the oven to 180°C and line the base and sides of an 18 x 18 cm slice tin with baking paper.

In a large bowl, mix the almond meal, half of the chopped macadamias, the mango, eggs, vanilla, macadamia nut oil and lemon myrtle. Pour the mixture into the prepared tin, then sprinkle the remaining maca nuts over the top.

Bake for 25–30 minutes or until the top is golden and a skewer inserted into the centre comes out clean. Leave to cool a bit before turning out onto a wire rack, then slice and serve cold for morning tea with a cuppa, or warm it up and serve with coconut ice cream for dessert. Yum!

Makes 9 pieces

I love hummingbird cake so much that it actually featured at my 21st birthday party. This muffin version is awesome. If you can't find fresh pineapple you can use the tinned stuff, but it's best to use fresh if you can. Don't forget you can freeze the muffins (without the spread) – I just put mine in an airtight container or zip-lock bags.

hummingbird MUFFINS

1½ cups almond meal
½ cup hazelnut meal
½ teaspoon ground cinnamon
¼ teaspoon ground nutmeg
½ teaspoon ground ginger
seeds of 1 vanilla pod (or ½ teaspoon vanilla powder)
pinch of salt flakes
3 eggs
¼ cup maple syrup
2 ripe bananas, mashed
½ cup medjool dates, pitted and roughly chopped
½ cup chopped fresh pineapple
1 cup roughly chopped pecans, activated if possible (see page 10)

Almond–ricotta spread

250 g ricotta
¼ cup maple syrup
2 tablespoons almond butter
¼ teaspoon ground cinnamon

Preheat the oven to 180°C and grease a 12-cup muffin tray.

Place the nut meals, spices, vanilla and salt in a large bowl and give them a good stir. Add the eggs, maple syrup and banana and mix well. Fold in the dates, pineapple and pecans until the mixture is evenly combined. Spoon into the muffin tray and cook for 40–50 minutes, or until the tops are golden. Leave to cool.

To make the almond–ricotta spread, combine all of the ingredients in a small bowl and beat until smooth.

When the muffins are cool, you can either ice them with the almond–ricotta spread (like cupcakes) or serve them split with a generous dollop of the spread. Store any leftover spread in the fridge in an airtight container for up to 5 days (I love it on a slice of paleo bread topped with sliced banana and cinnamon).

Makes 12

I've been making these choc cupcakes for yonks and they always deliver the goods. Here, I have topped the cupcakes with bee pollen. I love the added health benefits (amino acids and antioxidants) and the lovely bright colour. If you can't find bee pollen, desiccated coconut works brilliantly, too.

UNICORN cupcakes with bee pollen icing

- ½ cup coconut flour
- ½ cup cacao powder
- ½ teaspoon good-quality sea salt
- ½ teaspoon bicarbonate of soda
- 1 cup coconut sugar
- 6 eggs, at room temperature
- ½ cup coconut oil, melted

Icing

- 3 cups coconut sugar
- 100 g butter, softened
- ¼ cup nut milk (any kind, or use quinoa or rice milk if you prefer)
- ¼ cup bee pollen (or ¼ cup desiccated coconut), for decorating

Preheat the oven to 180°C and line one or two muffin or cupcake trays with patty cases.

Place the coconut flour, cacao, salt, bicarb soda and coconut sugar in a large mixing bowl and stir well. In a separate bowl, whisk the eggs and melted coconut oil. Add the wet ingredients to the dry ingredients and mix really well. Pour the mixture evenly into the patty cases. (You can fill them up to the top – they don't rise.) Bake for 15–18 minutes or until a skewer inserted into the centre of a cupcake comes out clean. Cool for 5 minutes in the tin then transfer to wire racks to cool completely.

To make the icing, place the coconut sugar in a food processor or high-powered blender and whiz to a fine powder. Place the butter in a large mixing bowl and beat until soft and pale. Gradually add the powdered coconut sugar and then the milk and continue beating until it's nice and creamy. Spread the icing onto the cooled cupcakes and sprinkle with bee pollen or desiccated coconut. I usually store these in an airtight container in the pantry, where they'll last for up to 4 days (if I can leave them alone!).

Makes 14–16

I made this crumble for my agent and friend Lee Lee, who just *loves* sweet spuds! It's really easy to make and tastes amazing. If you're not keen on using butter, coconut oil works equally well. (I love using butter, though, as it makes the crumble super crispy and the sweet potato deliciously creamy.)

sweet potato and pecan CRUMBLE

2 sweet potatoes (about 800 g), scrubbed and cut into 2 cm cubes
60 g unsalted butter, melted
½ cup coconut sugar
2 eggs
½ teaspoon ground cinnamon
¼ teaspoon ground nutmeg
pinch of salt flakes
coconut ice cream or yoghurt (optional), to serve

Crumble
½ cup quinoa flakes
½ cup pecans, activated if possible (see page 10), roughly chopped, plus extra
2 tablespoons almond meal
¼ cup coconut sugar
60 g butter, melted

Preheat the oven to 180°C and grease a 28 x 18 cm baking dish.

Bring 1.5 litres of water to the boil in a large saucepan. Add the sweet potato and cook for 20 minutes or until soft. Drain, then transfer to a large bowl and mash until you get the consistency you like. (I prefer a rustic lumpy mash, but make yours smooth if you prefer.) Add the melted butter, coconut sugar, eggs, spices and salt and mix well. Tip the sweet potato mixture into the baking dish.

To make the pecan crumble, combine all of the ingredients in a bowl and mix until nice and claggy. Spoon the mixture evenly over the sweet potato, then bake for 30 minutes, or until the topping is nice and crisp.

Allow to cool slightly, then slice and serve with a scoop of coconut ice cream or a dollop of coconut yoghurt and a pecan or two for garnish.

Serves 4–6

This is a true Super Crumble that not only tastes amazing but also gives you a hit of antioxidants and loads of good oils, protein and fibre from the nuts, seeds and oats. Try making it in individual ramekins – it makes an awesome breakfast.

raspberry, apple and ginger CRUMBLE

4 granny smith apples, cored and diced (I keep the skin on for extra chewiness)

1 cup fresh or frozen raspberries

1 tablespoon coconut sugar (or sweetener of your choice)

2 cm piece of ginger, grated

zest and juice of 1 lime

coconut ice cream or coconut yoghurt, to serve

Crumble

¼ cup quinoa flakes

¼ cup rolled millet

¼ cup almond meal

¼ cup shredded (or desiccated) coconut

½ cup chopped macadamia nuts, activated if possible (see page 10)

¼ cup coconut oil, melted

2 tablespoons coconut sugar (or sweetener of your choice)

Preheat the oven to 180°C.

Place the apple, raspberries, coconut sugar, ginger and lime zest and juice in a pie dish and get your mitts in there to gently coat the fruit with all the lovely flavours.

In a bowl place the quinoa flakes, rolled millet, almond meal, coconut and maca nuts and give them a good stir so they're well combined. Add the coconut oil and coconut sugar and rub it into the flakes with your fingertips to make a clumpy crumble. Spoon the crumble mixture evenly over the fruit and bake for 20–30 minutes or until the top is golden and the raspberries are oozing out a little bit.

Serve with your choice of coconut ice cream or yoghurt.

Serves 4–6

TIPS

To make individual serves, prepare the fruit mixture in a large bowl and then spoon it into four large ramekins (or six smaller ones). Top with the crumble and bake for 15–20 minutes or until golden.

Also, if you don't mind dairy, any unsweetened plain yoghurt (cow's, sheep's or goat's) works beautifully with this crumble, especially an organic full-cream version.

I've been seeing lots of delicious-looking but not-so-healthy sweet pizzas on social media for a while now, and it's been my dream to come up with a healthier alternative. Here it is! The base is like one giant, crispy pancake.

crispy dessert PIZZA

Base
1 cup buckwheat flour
1 cup almond meal
pinch of salt flakes
¼ cup coconut oil, melted
2 eggs, lightly beaten

Healthy 'Nutella'
1 cup hazelnut meal
⅔ cup cacao powder
pinch of salt flakes
½ cup maple syrup
3–4 tablespoons almond milk

Topping
½ punnet (125 g) strawberries
½ punnet (60 g) raspberries
½ cup almonds, activated if possible (see page 10), chopped
2 tablespoons flaked coconut

Preheat the oven to 180°C.

To make the 'Nutella', combine the hazelnut meal, cacao powder and salt in a bowl, then add the maple syrup and give it a really good mix. Gradually add the almond milk, stirring well in between additions, until you're happy with the consistency. Set aside.

To make the base, combine the buckwheat flour, almond meal and salt in a bowl. Using a wooden spoon, make a little well in the centre. Pour the coconut oil and eggs into the well and mix it up until you have a rough dough. Form the dough into two even-sized balls. Turn one ball out onto a sheet of baking paper on your work surface. Place another sheet of baking paper on top, then use a rolling pin or bottle to roll it out to a circle about 5 mm thick. Grab the edges of the baking paper and transfer the base (with the paper) to a baking tray or pizza tray. Peel off the top sheet and repair any tears in the base by smooshing the edges together with your fingers. Repeat with the other ball of dough and a second tray. Bake the bases for 10–15 minutes or until golden.

Remove the bases from the oven and spread a generous layer of healthy 'Nutella' evenly over the top, letting it melt in. Sprinkle over the berries, almonds and coconut. Slice and serve. Store the leftover 'Nutella' in a glass jar in the fridge for up to 2 weeks.

Makes 2

Combining apple crumble with cake makes for some pretty awesome magic, if you ask me. Try rolled oats instead of quinoa flakes and walnuts instead of macas. Both work a treat.

spiced apple crumble paleo CAKE

- ½ cup buckwheat flour
- ½ cup almond meal
- 2 teaspoons gluten-free baking powder
- ½ teaspoon ground cinnamon
- ¼ teaspoon ground nutmeg
- ¼ teaspoon ground star anise
- 4 eggs, whisked
- ¼ cup maple syrup
- 125 g butter (or 125 ml coconut oil), melted
- 1–3 tablespoons almond milk (if needed to get the desired consistency)
- 3 granny smith apples, unpeeled, cored and diced
- coconut or almond milk ice cream, to serve

Crumble

- ½ cup macadamia nuts, activated if possible (see page 10), roughly chopped
- ¼ cup quinoa flakes
- ¼ cup almond meal
- 60 g butter (or 60 ml coconut oil), melted
- ¼ cup maple syrup

Preheat the oven to 180°C. Line the base and sides of a round 22 cm cake tin with baking paper.

In a big bowl, combine the buckwheat flour, almond meal, baking powder and spices. Make a well in the centre and gradually add the eggs, stirring in little circles to coax the flour away from the sides of the well. Fold in the maple syrup and butter or coconut oil. If the mixture is too thick and doughy, add the almond milk 1 tablespoon at a time until you get a smooth batter. Fold through the diced apple. Transfer the mixture to the prepared tin and bake for 40 minutes.

To make the crumble, simply chuck everything in a bowl and mix well. Remove the cake from the oven after 40 minutes, sprinkle over the crumble mixture and return to the oven for a further 5–10 minutes, or until the top is golden and a skewer inserted in the centre comes out clean. This tastes absolutely delicious served warm with coconut or almond milk ice cream.

Serves 6–8

My dad *loves* his sweets (I wonder where I get it from!) and has a real soft spot for sticky date pudding and lemon butter. So I made this healthy combo just for him. Love you, Daddy-o! This recipe is equally delicious with limes in place of lemons. Also, don't worry if you forget to soak the nuts overnight – a 2-hour soak will do. And if you want to speed up the setting process, just put the finished pie in the freezer for 1 hour (instead of in the fridge for 2).

best ever raw lemon CREAM PIE

Base

- 1½ cups macadamia nuts, soaked for 2–3 hours (or overnight) then rinsed
- 1 cup desiccated coconut
- 8 medjool dates, pitted and soaked for 20 minutes in ½ cup water
- pinch of salt flakes
- 2 tablespoons coconut oil, melted

Lemon cream filling

- 2 cups raw cashews, soaked for 2–3 hours (or overnight) then rinsed
- zest of 1 lemon
- juice of 2 lemons
- 3 tablespoons maple syrup
- 1/3 cup coconut oil, melted
- pinch of salt flakes
- 1–3 tablespoons filtered water
- edible flowers (optional), to serve

Grease a 20 cm pie dish with a little coconut oil.

To make the base, just throw everything into the food processor, including half of the date-soaking water, and process until you get an even crumble. Pinch the mixture with your thumb and finger to test if it will stick together. If it's too dry, mix in a few more drops of the date-soaking water and check again. Repeat this process until it gets to the right consistency. Press the mixture into the base of the dish.

To make the filling, grab your food processor again and put in the cashews, half of the lemon zest (the other half is for garnish), the lemon juice, maple syrup, coconut oil, salt and 1 tablespoon of the filtered water. Process, gradually adding more filtered water, until the mixture is smooth and creamy. Tip the mixture into the pie dish, using a spatula to spread the filling over the base and making sure it is nice and even. Sprinkle the remaining zest over the top and refrigerate for 2 hours to set. Serve topped with edible flowers (if using). This will keep in the fridge for 4–5 days.

Serves 6–8

As a nutritionist, I work with people to help them reach their personal goals for health and physical wellbeing. And yes, diet is really important in terms of reaching those goals, but as we've seen earlier, it's harder to choose the right foods when we're tired, depressed or caught in a cycle of emotional eating. It's like a chicken—egg thing. If your head's not right, it's harder to make healthy food choices; yet if you don't eat real food, it can mess with your sleep and moods, keeping you in a negative feedback loop. One of the best ways I know to break out of this cycle is to nurture my soul.

For me, spirituality is being in touch with my deepest self; it's a sense of belonging and oneness with a universal intelligence or 'higher power'. For some people this means being part of a church, for others it's meditating every day or simply being in nature. All of these spiritual practices help us to feel peace and contentment by quietening our minds. Now not everything works for everyone, so don't throw in the towel just because your first experience with any of these practices was a dud. That's part of the process — keep going until you find what you love.

SOUL

> There's never nothing going on. There are no ordinary moments.
>
> Dan Millman, author and lecturer

MEDITATION

There are heaps of different styles of meditation, many of them based on the ancient practices of religions such as Buddhism, Hinduism, Taoism, Islam, Judaism and Christianity. Others, such as mindfulness meditation, are secular styles based on these traditions.

Meditation used to be considered totally hippie, but many counsellors, doctors and therapists now recommend it for reducing stress and helping with insomnia and anxiety. And because there are so many options, you're bound to find something that suits you. There are courses in traditional meditation, e.g. transcendental meditation (TM) or Vedic meditation, you can take guided meditations with any number of spiritual teachers (on retreats, online, buying CDs or DVDs), and there are even cool meditation apps.

When I did a Vedic meditation course, I learned a mantra (a special phrase) that I had to repeat over and over in my head for 20 minutes in the morning and 20 minutes at night. The idea is that the mantra blocks out your thoughts so that you can get into a really relaxed state. Then eventually the mantra floats away and it's just you. For me, 20 minutes twice a day is a bit tricky, so I try for at least 10 minutes and then do a whole bunch of other meditative activities (like yoga) to give my mind a rest and my spirit a boost.

Meditation tips

Pick a style that suits you

If you want to try meditation, it's important to pick a technique that works for you. We're all different, and while some people love the structure of going to classes or group meditation meetings every week, others are happier with an app they can use on the train on their way to uni or to work.

Make the time

You might start off really enthusiastic and determined, but like most things, daily meditation can be hard to stick to. A great trick my mediation teacher taught me was to do my meditation on the plane during take-off and landing. By the time the plane has taxied out on the runway and taken off (or landed and come in), I've usually had a lovely peaceful meditation session of at least 10 minutes, often more. This works really well for me. I love it! You can do the same on public transport.

Make a space

I think it helps to have a space in the house you can dedicate to mediation. Try not to make it in your bed, because ideally you want to be sitting upright so you don't fall asleep. I find sitting on a yoga block or bolster makes things comfy. Some people say it's best not to rest your back on something, but I find I can hold the sitting position longer when I have something to lean against, and the longer I am able to meditate the easier it becomes. Again, come back to whatever works for you.

Music

My meditation teacher tells me not to meditate with soft music in the background because it distracts my mind from my mantra. But sometimes, when I'm struggling to switch into the zone, I put on some super-mellow tunes and it helps.

Yin yoga

This is my favourite way to drop into the meditation zone. It's actually a form of yoga where you hold the poses for much longer — anywhere from 2—20 minutes (though usually around 5—7 minutes) — so that they are effectively a way of keeping both your body and mind very still. I love watching students float out after a good yin class — I call it 'yoga stoned'!

The name 'yin yoga' comes from the Taoist tradition. So while 'yang' relates to movement that creates heat in the body, 'yin' is about finding stillness and cooling the body, enabling you to stay in balance.

MINDFULNESS

So many of us live our lives at a hectic pace, multitasking as we rush to meet the next deadline, achieve the next goal or do the next thing on the list, and missing the whole journey. And we do this on autopilot, oblivious to the constant stream of chatter (self-talk) that is urging us on. Mindfulness helps us slow it all down by bringing our awareness to the present moment. We stop what we're doing for a moment (or two, or ten) and simply notice our thoughts, feelings and sensations, without judging them.

Mindfulness has been a core element of Buddhist practice for millennia and is increasingly being used in the West to reduce stress and treat a range of conditions, from anxiety and depression to addiction and chronic pain. Jon Kabat-Zinn devised his mindfulness-based stress reduction program way back in 1979, and it's now used all over the world in health clinics, schools, prisons, hospitals and other places.

Tips on being mindful

There's no need to spend stacks of money on courses or books in mindfulness (unless you want to). All you have to do is to take a moment to be still and observe your thoughts, emotions or sensations as often as you can. Some people like to do this at the same time every day, such as first thing in the morning or before they go to sleep. Others like to use environmental cues to help them practise mindfulness, such as when they're waiting for traffic lights to change, or standing in a queue, or waiting for the kettle to boil. The great thing is that every time you do it, you strengthen that pathway in your brain.

* Tune into your senses: what can you see? What can you smell or hear? Can you feel your clothes on your body?
* Close your eyes and see if you can 'feel' the energy in your hands.
* Notice your breathing: is it fast and shallow, or deep and long? Do you breathe out through your mouth or your nose? Close your eyes if it's hard to focus. Take three long, slow, deep breaths in and out through your nose.
* Where are your shoulders? Are they hunched up around your ears or are they dropped and relaxed?
* How do you feel emotionally? Do you feel calm or stressed?
* It sounds contradictory, but once you begin practising mindfulness and focus more on 'being' than 'doing', you'll be amazed at how productive you are. You'll get heaps more done from this chilled headspace than from buzzing around manically.

NATURE

Ever since humans began creating noisy, crowded urban environments, people have been heading into nature to recharge their batteries and de-stress. By nature, I mean natural environments such as mountains, forests, rivers, oceans or even deserts. Biophilia (one of my favourite words) takes that idea one step further by proposing that humans have an innate attraction to and love for nature, and that when we nurture that connection, it has a positive effect on our physiological and psychological wellbeing. In fact, there have been lots of studies on the positive effects of the natural environment on mental health and cognitive function. To me this makes total sense, because when I'm out in nature I feel calm and centred, and I have a clearer perspective on my life and a sense of the bigger picture.

The ocean

We are drawn to water – to lakes, rivers and streams, and especially the ocean. There's no doubt that a walk along the beach or a paddle or a swim is restorative and healing. Scientists think that this has something to do with the expanse of sky and water, which gives our brains a rest. And because we can float easily in saltwater, we feel light and free.

Some people believe that being near the water (especially moving water such as waves or a waterfall) exposes us to negative ions, and that these balance out the excess of positive ions we are exposed to when we spend so much time with computers, phones and other electronic devices. The scientific evidence behind this isn't all that clear, but that doesn't change the fact that being near water makes us feel awesome!

I try to get to the beach as much as possible in the summer months because I feel so centred and clear and rejuvenated there.

Camping

This has to be one of the most amazing ways to reconnect with nature, especially if you can give yourself a break from social media. And by camping I don't mean staying in a cabin or a camper van (though of course that's brilliant, too), I mean getting down on the ground and pitching a tent.

There's something special about being in physical contact with the earth (maybe that's why so many people love gardening). Some people even believe that the electrons from the earth's surface can get into our bodies and reduce stress and anxiety (they call it earthing). I'm not sure about the science, but it sounds lovely! And if you think about it, we do run about in bare feet when we go camping or go to the beach, and it does feel awesome to be in touch with the earth. Let Mother Nature work her magic on you, and if it's summer and a clear night (and it's safe), try sleeping out under the stars. It's pretty mind-blowing.

Mindful hiking

When I visited the Aro Hā health retreat in New Zealand, I went hiking in the mountains every day (the scenery was Lord of the Rings magical!) and for part of the time we kept a distance of 10 metres between ourselves and the next person. This was called mindful hiking because it enabled us to focus our attention on the hike itself, rather than chatting away to the person in front of us. I have to say that it was truly enriching: I noticed so many different sounds, I was more aware of temperature changes, and I just felt such a sense of tranquillity and connection to the earth. So now, whenever I go on a hike or even just walk, I take some time just for me to be at one with nature and to feel grateful that I'm healthy enough to be hiking in such stunning places.

Bring nature to your home or office space

Plants are the obvious way to bring a little bit of nature into an indoor environment. Some people love to have bowls of shells, rocks, pebbles or sand, which not only look great, but feel good to touch. Cut flowers are also awesome for bringing colour and freshness into your space. If I'm feeling a bit low, a bunch of blooms always makes me feel better, especially if they have a lovely scent as well.

Catch a few rays

One more thing: sunshine is an awesome healing force, so try to get a little each day. It helps to keep your mood pepped up and is brilliant in small doses for healthy skin.

Ways to get a nature fix in the city

If you're already an outdoorsy kind of person, then you'll know what to do and where to go! You don't need to spend loads of money or travel for hours to experience nature. I mean, even if you live in a city, there are always heaps of places that are little nature oases.

* Have a picnic in a park or a botanic garden.
* Lie on your back on some grass under a tree and look up through the branches. Your breathing rate will slow down, you'll inhale more deeply, and you'll start to feel a sense of clarity and peace.
* Read a book on a park bench.
* Ride your bike to the nearest river or lake.

Shells and pebbles not only look great, but feel good to touch.

Humans have an innate attraction to and love for nature.

Sunshine is an awesome healing force, so try and get a little each day.

Bring a little bit of nature into an indoor environment.

GARDENING

A garden can be your own little bit of nature, your own little sanctuary. It doesn't need to be massive – it can simply be a couple of pots, or if you live in an apartment, you can join a community garden. I have a windowsill herb garden, and it is so lovely to be able to pick fresh herbs for my cooking! But a garden is more than practical and useful: it is good for the soul. One Australian study found that people who participated in a community garden identified spiritual, physical and physiological benefits. If you don't have the space or you're not too sure where to start, here's a list of the 10 simplest herbs to grow.

Chamomile
Chamomile loves a sunny spot in the garden. The little flowers are very pretty and have long been used as a remedy for digestive problems, insomnia and menstrual disorders. To brew chamomile tea, simply pluck off a few flower heads and pop them in an infuser in a cup of boiled water. Leave for 3–5 minutes and enjoy.

Coriander
Coriander (cilantro) grows best if you plant it in early autumn or early spring as it loves cool, moist weather. If you plant it in summer it tends to bolt (go to seed) as a survival mechanism. The best way to slow it down is to plant your seeds in succession (every couple of weeks) so that as one plant bolts, the next is just starting to grow. I have mine in a medium-sized pot with lots of mulch to keep the soil cool. It's a delicious herb that goes well with any meat or salad, and also looks pretty spectacular.

Lavender
This amazing plant loves plenty of sunshine, well-drained soil and a moderate amount of water. Lavender has a long history of culinary, medicinal and household uses – everything from flavouring dishes (it is actually related to mint) to repelling insects. The oil has antiseptic properties that make it a great ingredient in natural cleaning products. It's also a calmative and has been used for anxiety, depression, tension headaches and insomnia. A few drops on your pillow at night will help you to fall asleep.

Lemon balm
Lemon balm thrives in sun or shade and has a similar spreading habit to mint. When you crush the leaves it smells wonderful (lemony with a hint of mint). It's been used in folk medicine for centuries to lift the spirit and calm the nervous system. You'll see it a lot in 'de-stressing' and calming teas. Brew fresh leaves in a cup of just-boiled water and try it yourself!

Mint
Mint thrives on water and will grow in the sunshine or shade. It also likes to take over the space where you plant it, so either keep it to just one pot, or a handy trick is to plant it in a pot and then put the pot into the garden bed so the roots don't spread out and take over the other plants. Then you'll have mint handy for fresh salads, marinades, tea and iceblocks in the summer!

Parsley
Curly-leaf parsley is easy to grow, though like mint it needs plenty of water. It's often used as a garnish, or when you need a stack of it in a raw dish like tabouli. There's also flat-leaf parsley, which has a stronger flavour and is used more in cooking. Both are high in vitamin C and a good source of iron. In folk remedies, parsley was considered an aid to youth and beauty. And there's another cool thing about parsley – the chlorophyll it contains can counteract the strong sulphur odours from onion and garlic – so chew a sprig if you've just had a garlicky meal.

Rosemary
Rosemary is amazingly drought tolerant and easy to grow from a cutting (it's better to break off a sprig at the point where it joins a larger branch). Just pop it in a glass of water and wait a week or two for little shoots to grow off the bottom, then plant it in soil and water well. You can use it fresh or dry. Some say it helps with memory – my mum used to put a sprig of rosemary into my school blazer pocket on exam days.

Roses
I know this doesn't seem like a herb, but the petals and seed pods (rosehips) have been used in herbal medicine for a long time. Rose-petal tea is said to lift the mood and, like chamomile, has also been used to help calm digestive issues. Rosehip oil has been used to soothe and repair damaged skin. In folk remedies, Roman women sprinkled themselves with rose petals after bathing and sucked on them to sweeten their breath. When growing roses, remember that they love water. Also, they are prone to attack by insects, mildew and other fungi, so you may need expert guidance to find non-toxic ways to promote healthy flowering.

Sage
Sage needs to be planted in a sunny position in well-drained soil. Most people know it as a delicious herb to use in cooking, but you can also use the leaves to make a tea when you have a cold; its expectorant properties help to clear the chest.

Thyme
Thyme is a hardy little groundcover plant and looks like a pretty green rug in your garden, with speckles of flowers in spring and summer. The leaves have antiseptic and antibacterial properties that help boost the immune system and protect against viral, bacterial and fungal infections. Try adding it to your next stew or winter soup.

KINDNESS

Being kind to people doesn't cost a thing but is incredibly enriching for both the giver and the receiver. There's been a lot of research on the psychology of giving, and it seems we're wired to help others. It was actually a survival thing for our ancestors to be empathic and caring to the members of their group because it helped them stay connected and therefore ensured their safety.

Many studies have found a direct link between performing kind actions and physiological and emotional health. Dr David R. Hamilton has found that acts of kindness create an emotional warmth that triggers the releases of oxytocin, the so-called 'love hormone'. The cool thing about oxytocin is that it triggers the release of nitric oxide, a chemical that dilates the blood vessels, reduces blood pressure and protects the heart. Other researchers have found that acts of kindness reduce anxiety in people with social phobia, as well as increasing their levels of wellbeing and happiness. I could go on and on!

Here are some of the random acts of kindness I do regularly. See if any of them sound like something you could do. And if you're already doing them, know that you are making the world an even more beautiful place.

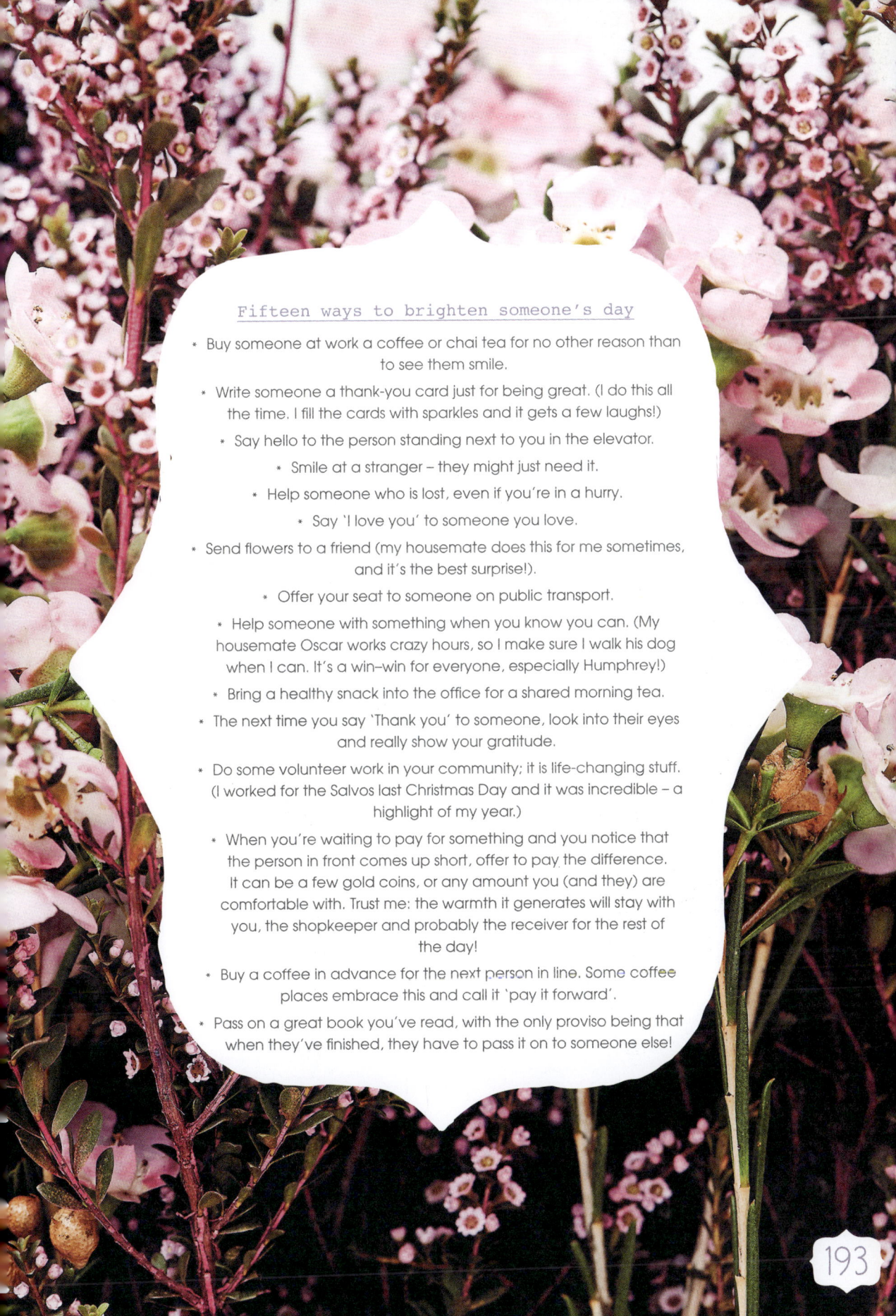

Fifteen ways to brighten someone's day

* Buy someone at work a coffee or chai tea for no other reason than to see them smile.
* Write someone a thank-you card just for being great. (I do this all the time. I fill the cards with sparkles and it gets a few laughs!)
* Say hello to the person standing next to you in the elevator.
* Smile at a stranger – they might just need it.
* Help someone who is lost, even if you're in a hurry.
* Say 'I love you' to someone you love.
* Send flowers to a friend (my housemate does this for me sometimes, and it's the best surprise!).
* Offer your seat to someone on public transport.
* Help someone with something when you know you can. (My housemate Oscar works crazy hours, so I make sure I walk his dog when I can. It's a win–win for everyone, especially Humphrey!)
* Bring a healthy snack into the office for a shared morning tea.
* The next time you say 'Thank you' to someone, look into their eyes and really show your gratitude.
* Do some volunteer work in your community; it is life-changing stuff. (I worked for the Salvos last Christmas Day and it was incredible – a highlight of my year.)
* When you're waiting to pay for something and you notice that the person in front comes up short, offer to pay the difference. It can be a few gold coins, or any amount you (and they) are comfortable with. Trust me: the warmth it generates will stay with you, the shopkeeper and probably the receiver for the rest of the day!
* Buy a coffee in advance for the next person in line. Some coffee places embrace this and call it 'pay it forward'.
* Pass on a great book you've read, with the only proviso being that when they've finished, they have to pass it on to someone else!

being with ANIMALS

Animals are such amazing friends. I love it when I get home from work and Humphrey is so excited to see me that he is wagging his tail like mad and running little marathons up and down the hall! Cats purr and headbutt us, or wind themselves around our legs. It feels great to be loved and wanted, and I truly believe that animals are here to teach us lessons of the heart.

You might think it's weird to be talking about animals when we're talking about health and happiness, but as you'll see, the bond we have with animals is much more than just fun: it promotes healing and wellness. My dad is a vet and he says that pets are incredible on many levels: they help us to relax, they are great 'listeners' and they get us outside in the sun and doing things like walking, running and playing games.

He says the therapeutic value of pets has been known for a long time. A study in the 1970s found that heart-attack patients who had pets lived longer than those who didn't, and another one found that petting a dog every day lowered blood pressure. In another study, AIDS sufferers with pets were 50 per cent less likely to report symptoms of depression. However, scientists have only recently begun to understand how this connection works.

When we cuddle and stroke our pets, it stimulates the production of the hormone oxytocin, which makes us feel happy and content and builds trust. (It's actually the same hormone that strengthens the mother–baby bond, and the bond between couples when they first fall in love.) As we saw in the previous section, oxytocin triggers the release of a chemical that reduces blood pressure. In another study, oxytocin was found to help wounds heal faster.

Pets for therapy is a widely recognised form of healing all over the world, and in Australia there are dozens of organisations that assist in the training of animals to take into hospitals, aged-care facilities, prisons, respite centres and even primary schools. Some schools, for example, are utilising the 'read to a dog' program to help young children who are have having difficulties learning to read, and they are finding that the dogs are helping far more people than just the children!

Our black labrador, Bobbie, visits a local aged-care facility, and I've been on some of those visits with my dad. It's so amazing watching the faces of the residents light up when they see Bobbie.

While dogs are more commonly used as therapy animals (simply because they are so easily trained), all sorts of other animals can be used as well, including cats, birds, horses and even dolphins. Equine-assisted therapy has been used for decades with disabled children, children on the autism spectrum and, more recently, psychotherapy patients to help them gain self-understanding and assist with emotional healing. Some therapists working with children have taken along cockatoos and bearded dragons to help the children relax and feel safe enough to share their thoughts and feelings.

If you can't have a dog or cat where you live, and you know you would love to have a pet, consider a smaller animal such as a guinea pig, a cockatiel, a budgie or even a rat (seriously, they don't smell at all and are curious and lots of fun!). Or volunteer at the nearest animal rescue centre (they survive on the generosity of people like you). You can also visit an animal sanctuary, or offer to house-sit for someone and look after their animals. If everything is too hard, then watch some of David Attenborough's documentaries – they are spellbinding.

This is the part where I share all of my favourite drinkable foods: smoothies, juices, fermented drinks and teas. If you think about it, drinks are a brilliant way to get even more nutrients into your diet: teas are brewed from medicinal (or just delicious!) plants, herbs and spices; juices are cleansing, phytonutrient-rich combos of raw fruits and veggies; and smoothies are protein powerhouses with their nut milks, seeds, fruit, veggies and yoghurt. Drinks are also quick to prepare and easy to experiment with. So have fun and get creative!

DRINKS

SMOOTHIES

Smoothies make the perfect 30-second meal if you're time poor but want to stay on the health train; maybe that's why I'm such a smoothie fiend! Texture is important. They need to be thick and smooth, which means blending them for just that little bit longer to get rid of any lumpy bits (though I don't mind nuts). Then I add some sparkle, an extra flavour twist or a little bit of crunch with a topping (see page 200).

smoothie TOPPERS

The idea behind smoothie toppers is to add texture, flavour and extra health benefits. The only rule is to use ingredients that you love! Here are some of the combos that I really like.

- White mulberries, pistachios and pumpkin seeds

- Shredded coconut, cacao nibs and goji berries

- Macadamia nuts, cranberries and sunflower seeds

- Bee pollen (it looks lovely and is full of amino acids and antioxidants) ...

- However, please be mindful that it takes a bee 8 hours a day for a full month to create just a teaspoon of bee pollen. Go easy.

- Almonds, cinnamon, desiccated coconut and sultanas

- Walnuts, cacao powder and orange zest

- Candied pecans (see page 30) or candied macadamias (see page 145)

I love having this green smoothie after my weight-training — the coconut water keeps it light, but it's still full of green goodness and fruity energy. When you're chopping the pineapple, don't forget to include the core, as it contains heaps of health benefits.

GREEN heavy lifter

- 1 cup chopped pineapple, plus extra wedges to serve
- handful of baby spinach leaves
- 2 cups coconut water
- 1 tablespoon coconut oil
- 1 tablespoon whey protein isolate (protein powder) (optional)
- 1 tablespoon shredded coconut

Pop everything into the blender and keep blending until you get the consistency you like.

Serve in tall glasses topped with shredded coconut and a slice of pineapple wedged onto the side (if you want to be 1980s fancy!).

Serves 2

The name says it all! The cacao nibs and macadamia nuts add a fun texture and crunchy contrast. You can also make this super thick like a chocolate mousse by using just 1 cup of almond milk (your serving size will be a bit smaller, of course).

CHOCOLATE brownie smoothie

- 1 frozen banana
- 1 tablespoon cacao powder
- ½ cup macadamia nuts, activated if possible (see page 10) plus extra to serve
- 1 tablespoon LSA (ground linseed, sunflower seeds and almonds)
- 2 cups almond milk
- 1 tablespoon maple syrup
- cacao nibs, to serve

Place the banana, cacao powder, macadamias, LSA, almond milk and maple syrup in a blender and process until you're happy with the consistency (I like mine with a few chunks of macadamia nuts through it).

Top with cacao nibs and a few extra macas, roughly chopped if you like.

Serves 2

I love the warming twang of the turmeric in this smoothie — you just know it's working its anti-inflammatory and antioxidant magic on you. If you like, you can cover any leftovers with plastic wrap and refrigerate to have the next morning. It may change colour a tad, but it will still taste unreal!

TURMERIC
anti-inflammatory smoothie

- 1 frozen banana or 2 frozen mango cheeks
- 2–3 cm piece of ginger, peel left on and scrubbed (or ½ teaspoon ground ginger)
- 2–3 cm piece of turmeric, peel left on and scrubbed (or ½ teaspoon ground turmeric)
- 1 tablespoon LSA
- ½ teaspoon ground cinnamon, plus extra for dusting
- 1 tablespoon coconut oil
- 2 cups almond milk

Pop all of your goodies into a blender jug and process until lovely and smooth.

Pour into glasses and top with a sprinkle of extra cinnamon.

Serves 2

This healing tea supports liver health with cleansing lemon and at the same time calms the digestive system with gentle chamomile. You can use any sweetener of your choice in place of the coconut nectar.

chilled-out chamomile tea SLUSHIE

2 cups chamomile tea, brewed for 5 minutes, cooled and chilled

1 peach, peel left on, stone removed

juice of 1 lemon

1 tablespoon coconut nectar

1 cup ice cubes

chamomile flowers and lemon zest, to serve

Place the tea, peach, lemon juice, coconut nectar and ice in a blender and pulse until smooth.

Serve topped with chamomile flowers and a pinch of lemon zest.

Serves 2

This smoothie is inspired by the hidden smoothie bowl places I visited on road trips I took in Hawaii. Honestly, they were some of the best smoothies I've had in my life! There's something magical about Hawaii and Hawaiian culture. The first time I visited, I cried as I left to go home. I remember the attendant checking my tickets saying, 'Don't worry – Hawaii will call you back. She has your heart.' How right she was! I've been back many times.

HAWAIIAN happiness

- 2 mango cheeks (fresh or frozen)
- ½ cup chopped pineapple (fresh is best)
- 1 frozen banana
- 2 cups coconut milk
- 1 teaspoon flaked or shredded coconut, to serve

Pop everything into the blender, blitz, then pour into glasses and top with some flakes of coconut.

Serves 2

TIP
If you're using fresh pineapple, keep the core when you're chopping it up as it contains bromelain, an enzyme with some pretty cool anti-inflammatory properties.

BLUEBERRY muffin smoothie

I love making smoothies that taste like a treat even though they're loaded with so many healthy goodies! This one is a real winner, especially with the crunchy topping. The blueberries pack a powerful antioxidant punch, and the nuts are a great source of protein and good fats.

- 1 cup frozen blueberries
- 1 cup cashews, soaked for 2–3 hours (or overnight) then rinsed
- 1 tablespoon maple syrup (or sweetener of your choice)
- seeds of ½ vanilla pod (or ¼ teaspoon vanilla powder)
- 2 cups nut milk (almond or hazelnut are delish)
- almond meal and dried blueberries, to serve

Place the frozen blueberries, cashews, maple syrup, vanilla and nut milk in a blender and process on high until smooth. Taste the smoothie and add a little more sweetener if you think it needs it (blueberries can vary in sweetness, depending on when they were grown and frozen).

Pour into tall glasses and top with a pinch of almond meal and a few dried blueberries.

Serves 2

This feels like you're having a treat when you're just having a super-thick, healthy smoothie! You can experiment with all kinds of toppings — macadamia nuts and goji berries work well, or even just a sprinkle of shredded or desiccated coconut.

choc mousse smoothie bowl with crunchy topping

1 avocado
2 frozen bananas
2 tablespoons cacao powder
2 tablespoons maple syrup, or sweetener of your choice

Topping
1 teaspoon cacao nibs
1 teaspoon white mulberries
1 teaspoon bee pollen (optional)

Pop the avocado, banana, cacao powder and maple syrup in the blender and process until super smooth. Pulse a couple of times to make sure you process any last little chunks of avo.

Combine the topping ingredients in a separate small bowl. Pour the smoothie into serving glasses and sprinkle over the topping.

Serves 2

TIPS
For the Bright Eyes, juice the carrots last so they help push the smaller things through. Also, the more lemon peel you use, the more bitter the flavour will be.

Keep the skin on the kiwis, carrots and lemon for more health benefits. If they're not organic, please give them a good wash.

JUICES

Juices are a brilliant way for our bodies to instantly absorb a concentrated hit of nutrients, and are very cleansing. I use a good masticating juicer (which retains some of the fibre), but you can also make juices in a super-gutsy food processor or blender the same way you make nut milk.

clean & GREEN

There's no fruit in here at all – just greens with a hint of ginger to make your tastebuds tingle. When I have this creation in my diet regularly, my eyes and skin are so clear and I just feel so energised!

handful of baby spinach leaves
2 celery stalks
2–3 cm piece of ginger
1 zucchini
1 cucumber

Pop everything in a juicer or high-powered blender, then pour into some pretty glasses and bottoms up!

Serves 2

bright EYES

Kiwifruit and carrots are good sources of vitamins A and C, both of which are needed for eye health. Plus you're getting a truckload of antioxidants with the lemon and ginger.

2 kiwifruit, roughly chopped (leave the skin on)
1 lemon, roughly chopped (keep some of the skin on if your juicer can take it)
2–3 cm piece of ginger, scrubbed but not peeled
2 large carrots, roughly chopped

Juice all your goodies, then enjoy. This one will keep for a few days in the fridge if you pop it in a sealed container.

Serves 2

This pretty juice is all about summer vibes. Sometimes I pop it in the freezer for 15–20 minutes so it goes a bit slushy. Or I crush half a cup of ice cubes and add them to the mix. Here's the juicy version!

2 cups roughly chopped watermelon (keep the rind on)
1 punnet (250 g) strawberries
handful of mint leaves

Pop through your juicer and enjoy!

Serves 2

The mint and pineapple in this recipe make a lovely flavour combo and are great for calming the digestion. Add the cucumber to your juicer last so it helps to push the mint through.

2 cups roughly chopped pineapple (include the core)
handful of mint leaves
2 cucumbers

Pop everything through the juicer and drink up!

Serves 2

TIP
For the Summer Sunset, add 1 lime (with some of the peel if you like) to give it a bit of kick.

FERMENTED drinks

Fermentation has been around for centuries as a means of preserving food and drink. The cool thing is that the friendly bacteria that do the fermenting are brilliant for gut health, which in turn boosts immune health.

KOMBUCHA

Kombucha is a super-healthy fermented drink brimming with probiotics. It starts out as a very sweet tea, to which we add a scoby (an acronym for 'symbiotic culture of [friendly] bacteria and yeast'), which looks a bit like a jellyfish pancake. The scoby feeds off the sugar in the tea, turning the tea into a fizzy, fermented, slightly sour drink. It's easier to make your own kombucha than you think, but you will need to get yourself a scoby. Jump online and suss out suppliers in your area, or just order one online. You'll also need some plain, organic store-bought kombucha. This recipe needs to be started 9–14 days in advance.

½ cup white sugar

4 organic teabags (black or a mix of black and green)

1 cup kombucha from a previous batch (or use organic, unflavoured store-bought kombucha)

1 scoby

For extra flavour

½ cup chopped fruit (peaches, strawberries, figs, apples)

pinch of ground spice (I love to add ginger, but you can try cardamom, cinnamon or even star anise)

Place 1.75 litres of water in a saucepan over a high heat and bring to the boil. Remove from the heat and stir through the sugar to dissolve. Pop in the teabags and leave them to steep for about 15 minutes. Meanwhile, sterilise a large wide-mouthed jar or ceramic bowl with boiling water.

Remove the teabags and transfer the sweet tea to the sterilised jar or bowl. Leave it to cool to just below body temperature (so it's lukewarm, not cold). Add the kombucha and then the scoby (don't worry if it sinks). Cover with a clean tea towel or a couple of layers of cheesecloth and leave to sit at room temperature for 7–10 days. (If your house is colder than 24°C, pop it on top of the fridge or near the dryer if you have one.)

Taste the kombucha after 7 days. If it has a good balance of sweet and sour and a nice bit of fizz, you can either bottle it as it is, or add some fruit and spices and ferment it for a bit longer. Either way, you first have to remove the scobys (there will actually be two, now: a 'baby' scoby will have formed on top of the 'mother'). Lift them out with clean hands and pop them into a glass container along with 1 cup of the liquid. (You can give one scoby away to a friend!)

If you want to add flavour, divide the rest of the kombucha between bottles with tight-fitting lids (glass or plastic is fine) and add your chosen fruit and/or spice. Make sure you leave at least 3 cm clear at the top for the extra fizz!

Leave the bottles at room temperature for 2–4 days, then transfer to the fridge. (You can either strain out the fruit and spices, or leave them in if you like a stronger flavour.)

Makes about 1.75 litres

Kefir is a fermented drinking yoghurt brimming with healthy yeast and bacteria. (It actually means 'feel good' in Turkish.) Although traditionally made from sheep's milk, goat's milk or cow's milk, you can also make non-dairy versions with coconut milk, nut milks or even soy milk if you're a soy fan. All you need is some 'kefir grains', which is the name given to the starter culture of yeast and probiotics (it has nothing to do with grains – the name comes from its appearance). These can be purchased from health-food shops or online. This recipe will need to be started 12–48 hours in advance.

KEFIR

1–2 tablespoons kefir grains

1 cup milk (any kind)

Pop the kefir grains into a glass jar, then add the milk. Cover the jar with clean cheesecloth or a paper coffee filter and secure it with an elastic band or string. Place in a warm spot for 12–48 hours, depending on how strong you like the flavour and how thick you want it to be.

When the milk thickens it's ready to drink. Simply strain out the grains and pop them into the next batch, or if you don't want to use them straight away, store them in the fridge in milk for a week.

Makes 1 cup

TIP
Don't heat or freeze your kefir grains as this can destroy them.

TEA

Tea is the most popular drink in the world — more people drink it than they do alcohol, coffee, soft drinks and flavoured milk put together! According to Chinese legend, Emperor Shennong (Shen Nung) discovered tea in 2437 BCE when a gust of wind blew a sprig of *Camellia sinensis* into his pot of boiling water. We've been drinking it ever since, steeping the dried leaves, fruits, flowers, bark and roots of different plants in hot water to hydrate, energise and heal ourselves.

Teas are a brilliant way to nurture and support your body. And there are just so many different teas, particularly the herbal teas or 'tisanes', which all have different properties. That said, herbs are pretty powerful and if you're not too sure about what's right for you, it's best to seek the advice of a health professional.

HERBAL TEAS

I love to experiment with different combinations. One of my favourites is a pretty mixture of lavender, rose petals and chamomile flowers, which I have before bed. I call it my 'love tea', but it's not what you might think! It's just about calming the nervous system right down so I get a peaceful night's sleep.

Some of the properties of different herbal teas

Calming
* chamomile
* lemon balm
* passionflower

Energising
* peppermint
* spearmint
* ginger
* green tea (note that this contains caffeine)

De-stressing
* lavender
* lemon balm
* oat grass
* passionflower
* ashwaganda (Indian ginseng)

Detoxing
* St Mary's thistle (milk thistle)
* nettle
* dandelion

Helping memory and concentration
* Brahmi (bacopa or Indian pennywort)
* rosemary
* gingko
* ginseng
* gotu kola

Aiding digestion
* peppermint
* chamomile
* ginger
* licorice
* fennel

Boosting immune function
* ginger
* thyme (for sore throat)
* sage (sore throat)
* licorice (sore throat)
* echinacea (immune stimulant)

Topical cold tea treatments
* puffy eyes (chamomile teabags)
* burns and scalds (chamomile teabags)
* cuts and wounds (chamomile teabags)
* sores and ulcers (chamomile teabags)
* mouth ulcers and bleeding gums (chamomile teabags)
* sunburn (chamomile teabags)

Other quirky treatments
* body odour (drink fennel tea to promote 'odourless perspiration')
* smelly feet (soak feet in a bucket of warm water with four teabags, the tannins in the tea help get rid of the nasty smell due to the astringent effect they have on the body)
* diarrhoea (tea tannins are astringent, helping shrink proteins in the gut and 'bind things up')
* hair loss (washing your hair in sage tea is said to prevent hair falling out!)
* hangover (ginger tea calms the gut)
* skin conditions (burdock root has been known to clear up psoriasis)

How to brew the perfect cup

* Start with a preheated pot or cup (fill your teapot/cup with hot tap water and let it stand for a minute).

* Fill your kettle or pot with *fresh* cold water. (In areas with poor-quality tap water, use bottled or filtered water. Do not use water from the hot-water tap.) Let the tap water run for a few seconds until it is quite cold. This ensures that the water is aerated (full of oxygen) and will release the full flavour of the tea leaves.

* Bring the water to a rolling boil. Don't let it boil too long as it will boil away the flavour-releasing oxygen.

* Pour boiling water over the tea leaves or teabag.

* Brew for 3–5 minutes (for green teas, the water should be a bit cooler and the tea steeped for 1–3 minutes).

Our friendships have a huge influence on our happiness. It's so important to have key souls around us who not only love us for who we are but also feel comfortable telling us when we stuff up. Being open to their points of view inspires us to grow.

Now this doesn't necessarily mean you have to have the same group of friends for your whole life — friendships ebb and flow. Some people come into your life for a short time and then leave — others are there for keeps. Don't be afraid of letting mates go. If they drift away, let them. Holding on to resentment or bitterness is not going to make them want to come back! I love that quote: 'If you love somebody, let them go, for if they return, they were always yours. And if they don't, they never were.'

Friendship has nothing to do with the number of mates you have (despite what social media might suggest). You can have one close friend and be just as happy as someone who hangs out with a dozen people or has hundreds of thousands of Instagram followers.

Friendship is a two-way connection, where both of you are enjoying and growing from the experience of being together. Some people say that they don't have a lot of luck with friendships, that their friendships always seem to be one-sided or their friends are always letting them down. I understand where they're coming from, but they're missing the point of friendship. There's a really old saying that to have good friends you have to be a good friend. If you want to attract kind and loving people into your life, you first have to be a kind and loving person.

Here are some of the things I've learned about friendship over the years. I'm no expert, but these work for me.

Listen mindfully

Truly listening to someone is one of the greatest gifts you can give. People want to be heard, and if you listen with all of your attention they feel valued and cared-for. So when someone is talking to you and you sense it is important to them, here are some tips for listening mindfully.

* Stop what you are doing. (Sometimes I'll be scrolling through Instagram and nodding as if I'm listening, but really I'm missing most of what the person is trying to tell me.) You need to learn to catch yourself in these types of situations, when you're not really there.
* Make eye contact with the person who is speaking and take a moment just to come back to now.
* Focus on what the other person is saying, not on what you are going to say next. (This is one of the hardest things to do; that's why you need to think of listening as a meditative practice so you can try to quieten your own noisy mind.)
* Ask questions to show that you are listening and communicate your genuine interest in the other person's story. And make sure your interest is genuine; people can quickly spot when you're faking it.

Be honest

When you are speaking to your friends, be honest about your thoughts and opinions. This doesn't mean you have to be bossy or insensitive, just assertive. It shows that you value yourself and gives others permission to do the same. Also, when you ask someone 'How are you?' or say 'Thank you', really mean it. Don't use them as throwaway lines. People can tell when you're being genuine.

Be kind

This one is a no-brainer, but it's amazing how many people don't put the effort into maintaining a friendship. If you love someone and you want to see them, does it really matter if you have to do the calling? Here are some little acts of kindness:

* Make a card and send it to them.
* Send them some flowers.
* Bring them a bunch of fresh herbs from your garden, or a freshly made batch of bikkies or energy balls.
* Remember their birthday.

Drop the expectations

This is such an easy thing to say and so incredibly hard to do. Most of us don't even realise we are doing it, but we are constantly expecting other people to behave in a certain way. We want our friends to be happy for us if we achieve success; we want them to call us and invite us to things; we want them to remember our birthday, to be kind to us, to be respectful … the list is endless. Yet we never stop and question why we have these expectations. The reason? So we will be happy! Isn't that crazy? We think we can't be happy if other people don't constantly show us their love and approval! The moment you expect something of someone, you're setting yourself up for the possibility of disappointment, so don't even go there. Just do your own thing and be kind, and then you'll attract the right souls into your life.

People say that romantic love is a 'cool, calm love'. When I first heard that expression, I thought no way! Surely true love is all about energy, passion and excitement. But the reality is that this crazy honeymoon phase doesn't last, and it's not supposed to. Instead, love becomes more comfortable, compassionate and caring — the stuff that lasts a lifetime. For me, real love is like a deep knowing and understanding of another soul.

VULNERABILITY

For many of us, our first experience of romantic love is bittersweet. On the one hand it's exciting and new and fun, but on the other, it often involves the pain and confusion of rejection. If you have been hurt, you might find it hard to let your guard down. You play it safe and keep people (especially potential partners) at arm's length. Unless we can allow ourselves to be vulnerable, to show our emotions and be open to the feelings of others, then we cannot truly connect with them. Vulnerability is the most important ingredient in a trusting intimate relationship.

How to tap into the real you

- Practise mindfulness: it will help you tune in to your thoughts and feelings (see page 185). But please be gentle with yourself. Don't judge those thoughts and feelings – just observe them. Once you begin to open your mind, your heart will follow.
- Tap into your spirituality in whatever way you love, whether that be yoga, walking in nature, being with animals, meditation, gardening, crystals or following an organised religion – there are no rules, only that you follow your heart.
- Tell someone how you feel: 'I love you', 'I love being with you', 'When I'm with you my heart is happy'.
- Apologise when you know you have behaved in an unkind or hurtful way. It doesn't matter who 'started it', or even what the other person did or said – apologise for your part and set yourself free.
- Listen to your partner if they want to talk about some behaviour of yours that is bothering them. Try not to immediately jump to defend yourself. You want someone who can challenge you, to help you grow. I'm not saying that you allow them to abuse you or anything, just that they can share with you when they feel you're being overly dramatic or negative or selfish or whatever. It's about finding someone who sees you for who you are and loves you for that but inspires you to be even more. That takes a truly open mind and heart.

When I was younger, I'd always be worried about being 'that girl' who orders gluten-free or dairy-free meals, or can't have this dessert or that piece of birthday cake. Going on dates was especially tricky. But you know what? I don't let this bother me anymore, and you don't need to either. The right person isn't going to judge you for that. They will accept you for who you are and support your choices. In fact, they may even be inspired to try some of your food for themselves.

I once dated a DJ who wasn't into health at all, but within a year we were going to raw food prep school together and whipping up green smoothies for brekkie each day. I didn't lecture him or push him or anything – I just lived it, and I guess he could see that I was having loads of fun so he wanted to share it with me! So live your life the way you love to; own it. Be that person who orders tea instead of wine on your first date (I did!) – honour and respect yourself from the very beginning.

And this works the other way, too.

Adventures

It seems a bit silly to say that the strength of your relationship also depends on your shared experiences, but some people forget this, especially after the honeymoon period. You do need to keep going on little fun adventures with each other, because they are the glue that keeps your connection strong. Keep challenging yourselves so that you have stories to share: 'Remember when we …'

Shared values

Values is a big one. For a relationship to be lasting, you and your partner need to have similar values; you need to share similar belief systems about how the world works and how you see your place in it. This is the big-picture stuff like politics, religion, child rearing and social justice. It's fine if you have different tastes, interests and opinions (in fact, it's more fun because you get to learn from each other), but unless you share core beliefs, you can't truly connect.

I've been in this situation myself. Once the dreamy honeymoon phase wore off, I just felt in my heart that the relationship wasn't right – we had such different views about things. I still loved and cared for him, but I knew our values didn't match up. It was really hard to leave, but in the end I had to do it to set us both free.

dealing with CONFLICT

The occasional argument is a normal part of any relationship and offers you not only the opportunity to learn more about each other, but also to grow as individuals. Every compromise, every resolution is a positive step forward. However, if you are constantly arguing without being able to resolve any issue and one of you is yelling, slamming doors or becoming abusive, then you need to get help.

An argument usually occurs when two people have different beliefs about what should or shouldn't happen and each of them feels personally threatened by the other's point of view. I know that sounds a bit silly, especially when we're such social beings and need to be in relationships, but we're hard-wired for survival. When our brains detect a threat (whether it's real or imagined), they automatically prepare us to fight, run away or play dead ('fight, flight or freeze'). That's why our hearts race, our faces go red and we can find ourselves lashing out verbally, running to another room or shutting down and refusing to talk to the other person.

Conflict also triggers our hunger hormones (to give us the energy to fight or outrun the 'danger' our brains think we're facing). This is why many of us are inclined to want to eat sugary, high-energy foods if we've just had a blue with someone.

Lots of people simply dump their partners if they experience a lot of conflict, but it actually takes two people to have an argument, and whatever triggers you have in your current relationship will still be there in the next one. Consider talking to a therapist or getting some other kind of help to identify what's going on underneath so you can break out of your old patterns. Don't be ashamed to ask for help. It's not a sign of weakness but of real courage.

BREAK-UPS

Let's not beat around the bush here: break-ups suck. Whether you're the one who's been dumped or you initiated the split, on some level everyone gets hurt.

In the past when I've gone through a break-up, I've eaten lots of unhealthy chocolate and listened to super-amazing but quite melancholy music (think Bon Iver and The National on repeat). I'd feel high for about 20 minutes (as the sugar did its thing and hit the reward centre in my brain), then as I 'came down' the feeling of flatness and self-loathing would arrive, and I would crave more sugar. (See Emotional Eating on page 56.)

I know I'm not alone here. Most of my clients talk about a particular food they use to make themselves feel better — that one thing that just hits the spot, giving their brains the phenylalanine and dopamine jump they crave. It's very short-lived, but it's that same feeling we get when we're in love.

The problem is that once you've gone nuts on sugary junk, you may put on weight, which makes you feel even worse about yourself, so you keep reaching for the sugar and get caught in a vicious cycle.

Fortunately, I've learned from past experience that the emotional pain will dissipate. Every day gets a little bit easier, especially if I am kind to myself. And one of the kindest things of all is to honour my sadness. I don't try to fight it: I let myself feel it then I let it go. It's so empowering when you actually sit in the pain and don't resist it. I find I move through it much faster than when I try to stop it. Some people think sadness is a negative emotion, but I think of it as an opportunity for growth. There is always a great lesson for me to learn that inspires me to follow my dreams.

Figuring out what to do with your life can seem overwhelming, especially when you're young and feeling pressure from everyone around you to make a decision about what career path to take.

One thing that really helps is to identify the activities that put you in 'flow'. This means you become so absorbed in them that you lose all track of time: it could be writing, photography, painting, designing something on the computer, public speaking, technology or being around animals. Then, once you've found the things that bring you flow, take small steps towards doing more of them. This in turn will make you happier and more productive in all the other areas of your life. The more you are in flow, the more things will fall into place.

When you love your job, it's not really 'work' — it's a joy, and you're willing to put your heart and soul into it.

For years I was working at a juice bar or health-food store, teaching lots of yoga (about 28 classes a week at one stage), or taking nutrition consultations to make ends meet. The truth was I was burning out and I wasn't getting any spare time to film or write, which were passions I really wanted to explore. So I took a leap of faith and decided to drop my food-service jobs and only teach yoga for larger groups and take consults on a case-by-case basis. I was on my own. I knew I was taking a risk, but it just felt right. I knew what I wanted to do and I loved every minute of it.

Within two months I had released a skincare product, Oscar Youth Elixir (named after my roommate), which sold out in three days. I kept going from there, focusing on my books and films and doing everything I could to realise my dream of helping people take charge of their health and happiness. It was amazing — people just kept coming into my life at the right moment to help and soon I had a great team who believed in my dream as much as I did.

CAREER

> I have found the most success when I followed my gut. Never underestimate the power of intuition.
>
> — Liesel Jones, Olympic gold medallist

OPPORTUNITY

An opportunity is a set of circumstances in time that allow you to do something. It might be something you hadn't ever thought of doing, or something you've always wanted to try but fear stopped you. When things come your way, trust that they are here for a reason and go for it. Opportunities will always help you to grow, to change, to learn new skills or to improve on old ones. And the stuff-ups are your greatest teachers!

Sometimes we can be so caught up in trying to control what happens in our life that we don't even notice when opportunities arise. Or if they do, we instantly talk ourselves out of them. It takes an open mind to recognise them, and an open heart to give them a go. Yes, it might be out of your comfort zone, or even downright scary, but that's perfect. A little bit of fear gives you the adrenaline and focus to do what needs to be done.

Last year I got the opportunity to skydive. It had always been a dream of mine, so I said yes even though I was terrified. I mean, I was so nervous that every time I talked about it my palms would go all sweaty. On the morning of the jump, I was so anxious that my mouth completely dried up. But as soon as I got into the plane I told myself, 'Wow! I am so grateful for this experience and I'm going to soak up every single second!' And I did.

Don't let your fears hold you back. If it feels right in your heart then go for it. Opportunities come in all shapes and sizes and if we're too scared to give them a shot we'll miss the boat.

how to make a DREAM BOOK

One way to help you recognise opportunities is to stay in touch with your dreams. I don't mean the dreams that you have while you're sleeping, but the daydreams you have about how you see your life unfolding and what you want to achieve. I made my first dream book when I was 21 — I've made six since then — and it's amazing to look back and see the progress I've made. Here's how I make mine.

First up, I get a blank notebook — not too big so I can carry it around with me — and a few different-coloured pens that feel good to write and draw with. I also grab a couple of my favourite magazines, some good scissors and a glue stick.

Next I find a nice spot to work. Sometimes it's out in nature, but it might also be a corner of the kitchen table. Then I pop on some tunes and get comfy.

Then I just start drawing, writing, doodling and cutting out images or words from the mags. I don't think about it — I just let my heart show me what to do. I glue the words and images onto the pages in any old way. (I love how tactile this is — it's so different from working on screens, and I reckon it gets me in touch with my deepest creative self.) This is how I start, then I just keep adding to the pages. I work on it for as long as it feels right, putting it aside when the natural flow is gone. Some days I spend five minutes on it and others I spend hours.

My biggest tip? Keep it personal and keep it just for you. That way you can let your guard down and create something that really inspires you and lights your soul.

Ideas for your dream book

There are no rules here: anything goes! I press flowers into my dream book, I put plane tickets and gig tickets in there, I write recipes in there and glue in little love notes I've received. Here are some more ideas.

- Trips you'd like to take
- Your career goals, broken down into short-term, medium-term and long-term ones
- Your values
- The qualities and values of your ideal partner
- Your favourite quotes
- Affirmations (positive and in the present tense), such as: 'I am happy', 'I am beautiful', 'I am kind'

If, like me, you love making lists, research says our brains respond better to colouring in a box rather than ticking or crossing off something on a list. Apparently it activates the reward pathway in the brain, which helps keep us motivated to colour in those boxes!

One of my best mates, Karina, once said to me, 'Lola, you can be healthy anywhere, and you can be unhealthy anywhere.' That's so true, yet sometimes I think we use travel as an excuse to ditch our health goals.

'I'm on holidays!' people say. 'I deserve this!' Sure, it's great to try new foods and to enjoy the occasional treat, but if your holiday morphs into one big indulgent foodie adventure it can be really hard to get back on the healthy eating wagon when you're home.

Then there's business travel where you're in transit a lot of the time or on a tight schedule between meetings or events, and it's almost impossible to have a 'routine'. I know this situation well, and the best solution is to be organised. The following tips will help you stay on track.

TRAVEL

> The journey of a thousand miles begins with a single step.
>
> Lao-Tzu, philosopher

FOOD

* Pack snacks like nuts, dips, veggie sticks and fresh fruit for the plane. (Airline food is not a great idea, even if you don't follow a strict paleo eating plan or have food allergies!) Just remember that you will have to eat what you bring or throw it away due to quarantine regulations.

* Pack some staples that don't need refrigeration and don't break any quarantine rules. I pack oats, chia seeds, nuts, raw chocolate and protein powder, so I know I have a brekkie ready to go if I'm really stuck or have a super-early start. I also bring dukkah, ras el hanout or another favourite seasoning for my salads. And of course I pack my own teabags; I love being able to curl up in bed with my favourite sleepy-time herbal tea.

* If you have meetings or events where you have to eat out, that's fine — just keep it nice and simple: protein and veggies. And ask for sauces on the side if you're not sure what's in them.

* If you're eating in, research local healthy eating spots (such as organic grocers and health-food stores), farmers' markets or just supermarkets. If there isn't anywhere with healthy food, I go to the local supermarket to get a few salad ingredients, avocados, some tinned tuna and some almond milk for my brekkie. I ask at reception for a bowl, a knife and a fork and make a little tuna salad with fresh leaves, lots of avo and a pinch of spice mix or seasoning.

* Stay hydrated. I find that a lot of flying dries my skin, so I always pack a jumbo-sized bottle of water and use a little extra moisturising oil.

SLEEP

This can be tricky, especially on long-haul flights, but try not to travel exhausted. When we are tired it's much harder to resist the unhealthy treats in a hotel minibar (or indeed wherever we are). Have a bath (if your room has one) or just take the opportunity to go to bed early and have a good sleep — think of your hotel stay as a 'mini retreat'.

EXERCISE

Pack your runners. There might be a decent gym in the hotel, so make use of it (if that's your thing). Better still, get up early and go for a walk or a run — it's a great way to explore a new place. I always go for a run in a new city because there's so much to be seen and discovered, and it always puts me in a positive mood for the day!

SOUL

* If you're on holiday or you have some free time in your work schedule, then think about booking a massage, a facial or even a manicure — just something that's a little gift for you.
* Research the nearest yoga studio and ask about taking a casual class, or simply do a Salute to the sun A (see page 122) or another routine you love in your hotel room. I do yoga in my hotel room *all* the time!
* Find out if there are parks or nature reserves nearby and go exploring.
* Do a social-media call-out: ask your mates about the top attractions to see and the top activities to do.

THANKS

Mary Small, for bringing this dream to life and really letting it be full of heart. I really value you and your belief in me. It's an honour to work with you.

Lauren Miller Cilento, you have worked so hard to make all of these dreams come true. Your support means loads and your fashion-styling trips are my favourite.

Lee Lee Sutherland, you've become such a great friend and I am loving seeing your journey unfold. You are one inspiring soul.

Marlene Richardson, for taking me under your wing. You've been unreal to work with.

Tallulah McAloon, for always being such a positive soul and helping manage all my stuff!

Clare Marshall, it's been such a joy to bring this together. I love how chilled you are and how comfy you make me feel when we're shooting. Thank you so much.

Charlotte Ree, you are such a pocket rocket. You always give it your all and it shows in the amazing work you do. Thank you!

Linda Raymond, Lindi-Lou, you have been my rock since the beginning and you have such a real heart. Thank you for always being so honest with me, it means so much.

Daddy-o, for always telling me to go after my dreams, no matter how big they are.

Mum, for being my number-one supporter and always helping to spread the love. It means loads.

Tristo, my baby bro, for being such a champion and a solid support. Thank you … for looking after Humph, too!

Hayley Van Spanje, your advice is brill and always on point. Thank you!

Michelle Mackintosh, I love every single second of working with you. You are such a talented soul.

Miriam Cannell, you are a such an awesome editor and you are so kind and gentle with my words. Thank you for really honouring my wishes and making this book the best it could be.

Karina Duncan, KD, you are a special soul. Thank you for always being there, and for being such a styling whiz – love watching you in your element!

Eve Wilson, it's been unreal to work with you. You have really created magic here.

Rochelle Seator, you were a dream to work with. Thank you so much!

Emma Warren, you make me smile so much on set. Always an honour, Guapa.

Emma Christian, you are a sweet soul and always light up a room. Can't wait to work together again!

Hannah Marshall, I love every second we get to work together. Let's do more of it!

Emma van Leest, for your creative genius and stunning artwork. I really appreciate all the love and passion that has gone into making these magical, whimsical masterpieces.

Belinda Zollo, thank you so much for teaching me my new mantra: 'me first, then you first.'

Jaidyn Thompson-Kemp, thank you for helping with my makeup on cover day and sharing your stories.

Tim O'Keefe, you are the best – it's that simple. Love your work and trust everything you create.

Thank you so much to the labels who helped dress me for this shoot: **Husk**, **Tluxe** and **Steele**.

Tre Dallas, thank you so much for pulling together so many outfits for this shoot. You were a huge help and always make me smile.

Arro Home, Bonnie and Neil, Home-work and **Kaz Morton**, thank you for your ace creations. I am blown away by what you come up with and love working with you.

Rebecca Rich, thanks for being such an ace recipe tester and giving it to me straight. I value you loads!

Thanks to **Jad Patrick**, my hobbit bud who always sees the lightness in any situation.

Thanks to **Mel Tjoeng**. Love creating magic with you, Mellie.

Power Living, thank you for letting us shoot the yogi stuff at your awesome Fitzroy studio. Loved it!

Rivis Donnelly, you always spread the love and I am very grateful. Can't thank you enough.

Charlie Goldsmith, I'm always your number-one spud.

Leisel Jones, you're a real mate. You are so down-to-earth and you always crack me up.

Faustina Agolley, you've not only been a huge support you're also an ace friend. So grateful to have you in my life.

Dan Adair, you're the best PT and you truly inspire me to raise the bar.

Lisa Mitchell, my whimsical bud, love seeing you shine.

Maddie Dixon, keep living from the heart. That's where the magic is, my friend.

Sophie Ball, you always speak the truth and you're a real mate. Thank you.

Andrea Evans, A. Apple, so much time can pass but nothing changes, you are one unreal soul.

Dexter Gordon, you are a champion and so kind. Thank you, Dex.

Alastair McCausland, I've loved working with you. You're an ace soul.

Avis Cheung, thanks for always having my back.

Chris Wilson, thanks for helping me grow as a yoga teacher. I have never thanked you before, but you've been a huge influence on me, and I can't thank you enough.

Hugh Lee, my yin teacher inspiration, you truly live your bliss.

Lucy Roach, thanks for taking that very first chance on me.

Aro Hā, thanks for the sweet New Zealand yogi photos. Your place is magic.

Mietta Gornall. Oh, Miets, you are such a ray of sunshine.

Kane Dignum, thanks for being the first person to truly inspire me.

Thanks to all the yoginis who participated in my class for the book shoot: **Sharon Brooks, Phoebe Cole, Ashleigh Dickinson, Emily Dowling, Hugh Lee, Maud Léger, Brooke Luty, Kathy Peterson, Annabel Reiter** and **Ayami Urli**.

INDEX

A
acceptance and commitment therapy (ACT) 52
addictions 16, 52
adventures 243
airline snacks 262
almond butter 8
almond meal/flour 8
almond milk 8
Almond–ricotta spread 165
amaranth 8
animals 195
apologising 240
apples
   Apple pie oats in a jar 28
   Brekkie crumble 38
   Raspberry, apple and ginger crumble 170–1
   Spiced apple crumble paleo cake 174
artificial sweeteners 18
assertiveness 59, 60, 234
avocados 8
   Avocado dressing 71
   avocado oil 8
   Barramundi with summery salad 109
   Choc mousse smoothie bowl with crunchy topping 214
   Foodie facial 135
   Grapefruit and avo salad 92
   Mexicana avo salad 88

B
bananas
   Choc mousse smoothie bowl with crunchy topping 214
   Chocolate brownie smoothie 204
   Paleo banana and cranberry bread 40–1
   Turmeric anti-inflammatory smoothie 207
Barramundi with summery salad 109
bathroom cleaner, homemade 137
Beanie brownie 160–1
bedtime rituals 130
bee pollen 8, 200
Bee pollen icing 166
Beetroot gravlax with creamy mustard sauce 106–7
Best ever raw lemon cream pie 176
Bikram yoga 118
binge eating 56
biophilia 186–7
black beans 8
   Beanie brownie 160–1
   Mexicana avo salad 88
black peppercorns 8
Blueberry muffin smoothie 212
body odour 227
break-ups 246
breakfast 26
Brekkie crumble 38
Brekkie salad with poached eggs 47
Bright eyes 216–17
Broccoli 'couscous' salad 84–5
buckwheat 8–9, 12
   Crispy dessert pizza 173
   Sticky date pancakes with coconut yoghurt 36–7

C
cabbage
   Cheat's kimchi 76–7
   Chunky health nerd soup 96
   Simple sauerkraut 78
   Summer slaw with blueberries and homemade mayo 81
cacao 9
cakes
   Spiced apple crumble paleo cake 174
   Unicorn cupcakes with bee pollen icing 166
calming herbs 227
calorie-counting 22
camping 187
carbohydrates 116–17
cardio training, foods for 116–17
career path 248, 256
carrots
   Bright eyes 216–17
   Carrot cake cookies 155
   Carrot cake paleo pancakes 34
cauliflower, Whole roasted, with almond butter sauce 94
chamomile 191
Cheat's kimchi 76–7
cheese *see* feta; ricotta
chia seeds 9
Chicken, mushroom and quinoa risotto 104–5
chickpeas
   Chunky health nerd soup 96
   Green hummus 86–7
Chilled-out chamomile tea slushie 208
chillies 9
Choc mousse smoothie bowl with crunchy topping 214
Chocolate brownie smoothie 204
cholesterol 22
Chunky health nerd soup 96
Cinnamon coconut sugar 148
Clean & green 217
cleaning products 137
coconut
   coconut flour 9
   coconut milk/cream 9
   coconut oil 9, 135
   coconut syrup 9
   coconut water 9
   dried coconut 9
coconut sugars
   Cinnamon 148
   Ginger 149
   Lime 148
   Pumpkin pie spice 149
   Vanilla 149
coincidences 250
concentration, herbs for 227
confidence 59, 60, 62
conflict resolution 244
cookies
   Carrot cake cookies 155
   Pumpkin pie cookies 156–7
core values 64–5, 243
coriander 191
cosmetics 132

Crispy dessert pizza 173
Crispy salmon with grapefruit and avo salad 92
crumbles
    Raspberry, apple and ginger crumble 170–1
    Spiced apple crumble paleo cake 174
    Sweet potato and pecan crumble 168
crystals 140

D
daily eating 25
dates, medjool 9, 142
    Best ever raw lemon cream pie 176
    Sticky date pancakes with coconut yoghurt 36–7
de-stressing, herbs for 227
detoxing, herbs for 227
diabetes 16, 22
diarrhoea 16, 18, 227
digestion, herbs for 227
dopamine 16, 18
dream books 254–6
dressings
    Avocado dressing 71
    Homemade mayo 81
    Miso dressing 98
    Waldorf dressing 82
drinks 196
    see also juices; smoothies; teas

E
eating out 262
eggs 10
    Brekkie salad with poached eggs 47
    Green shakshuka 48–9
    Rainbow yoga bowl with green hummus 86–7
    Salmon, kale and dill omelette 50
Emmami salad 98
emotional eating 56, 178, 246
endocrine disruptors 138
endorphins 116
energising, herbs for 227
ethical food 22
exercise 22, 112, 116–17
    while travelling 264
expectations, of friends 234
eyes, lines around 135

F
failure 62, 66
fats 22
    the good kind 135
fermented drinks
    Kefir 222–3
    Kombucha 221
fermented food 12
    Simple sauerkraut 78
feta
    Green shakshuka 48–9
    Mushroom, feta and pine nut muffins 74
figs
    Halva brain balls 150
fish
    Barramundi with summery salad 109
    Beetroot gravlax with creamy mustard sauce 106–7
    Crispy salmon with grapefruit and avo salad 92
    Emmami salad 98
food cravings 16, 18
Foodie facial 135
friendship 230, 234
fructose 22

G
gardening 190–1
Ginger coconut sugar 149
Gingerbread porridge with candied pecans 30
glucose 16, 22
goji berries 10
gratitude 66, 115
Green heavy lifter 202
Green shakshuka 48–9
Green hummus 86–7
grieving 66

H
hair, foods for 135
hair loss 227
hair products 132
hair treatment, Super-natural 135
Halva brain balls 150
hangover 227
happiness 6
Hawaiian happiness 210–11
headaches 18
healthy body 112, 115
herbal teas 11, 224, 226, 228
    brewing the perfect cup 228
    properties 227
    topical cold treatments 227
herbs 10, 191
Homemade mayo 81
honesty 234
honey, raw 10, 142
Hummingbird muffins 165
hydration 18, 262

I
immune function, herbal teas for 227
ingredients, essential 8–11
integrity 64
intimacy 236, 240
    see also relationships
intuition 6, 140

J
juices 196, 217
    Bright eyes 216–17
    Clean & green 217
    Minty cleanser 218
    Summer sunset 218–19

K
kale
    Brekkie salad with poached eggs 47
    Emmami salad 98
    Kale nut butter 42–3
    Kale Waldorf salad with real mayo dressing 82
    Porterhouse with kale and sweet spud mash 110
    Pumpkin and millet risotto 100–1
    Salmon, kale and dill omelette 50
    Sweet spud and kale bites with avocado dressing 71
Karina's pretty raspberry and coconut slice 158
Kefir 222–3
kindness 192–3, 234
Kombucha 221

L

labels on packaging 22, 137
lavender 191
lemon
   Best ever raw lemon cream pie 176
   Lemon cream filling 176
   Lemon and lime protein bites 152
lemon balm 191
Lime coconut sugar 148
linseed (flaxseed) 10
listening, mindful 234, 240
liver function 22
loaves
   Paleo banana and cranberry bread 40–1
   Pumpkin and zucchini loaf with minty ricotta spread 44–5
love 236, 238, 240
LSA 10

M

macadamia nuts 10
   Best ever raw lemon cream pie 176
   Broccoli 'couscous' salad 84–5
   Mango, macadamia and lemon myrtle slice 162
   Maple macadamia nut butter 146–7
   Salted caramel and cinnamon macadamias 145
macadamia oil 10
Mango, macadamia and lemon myrtle slice 162
Maple macadamia nut butter 146–7
maple syrup 10, 142
mayo, Homemade 81
meal-planning 24
meditation 182–3
medjool dates 9
memory, herbs for 227
Mexicana avo salad 88
microwave ovens 138
millet 10
   Millet and pumpkin risotto 100–1
mindful eating 24
mindful hiking 187
mindful listening 234, 240
mindfulness 52, 185, 240
mindset 52, 54, 59, 66
mint 191
   Minty cleanser 218, 219
   Minty ricotta spread 44
Miso dressing 98
mistakes, learning from 62, 250
Moroccan nights veggies 102–3
muffins
   Hummingbird muffins 165
   Mushroom, feta and pine nut muffins 74
   Paleo pumpkin muffins with kale nut butter 42–3
mushrooms
   Mushroom, chicken and quinoa risotto 104–5
   Mushroom, feta and pine nut muffins 74
   mushrooms, cleaning 105
myelin 22

N

nature 186–7, 265
neuroplasticity 52
nourishment 16, 22
nut milks 10, 22
nuts 10
   candied 30

O

oats 10
   Apple pie oats in a jar 28
   Brekkie crumble 38
   Gingerbread porridge with candied pecans 30
olive oil, extra-virgin 10–11, 135
omega-3 oils 135
omelette, Salmon, kale and dill 50
opportunities 253
overeating 24
oxytocin 192, 195

P

Paleo banana and cranberry bread 40–1
paleo principles 12, 166
Paleo pumpkin muffins with kale nut butter 42–3
pampering oneself 265
pancakes
   Carrot cake paleo pancakes 34
   Sticky date pancakes with coconut yoghurt 36–7
parabens 132
parsley 191
peppercorns, black 8
PET bottles 138
pineapple
   Green heavy lifter 202
   Hawaiian happiness 210–11
   Minty cleanser 218
   pineapple cores 211
pizza, Crispy dessert 173
plastics 138
pomegranate 11
Porterhouse with kale and sweet spud mash 110
pumpkin
   Paleo pumpkin muffins with kale nut butter 42–3
   Pumpkin and millet risotto 100–1
   Pumpkin pie cookies 156–7
   pumpkin seeds 11
   Pumpkin and zucchini loaf with minty ricotta spread 44–5
PVC (polyvinyl chloride) 138

Q

quinoa 11, 12
   Mushroom, chicken and quinoa risotto 104–5
   Quinoa chocolate risotto 33
   Quinoa surprise slice 72

R

Rainbow yoga bowl with green hummus 86–7
Raspberry, apple and ginger crumble 170–1
real food 12, 14, 22
recipe notes 8, 68
relationships 236, 238, 240, 243, 244, 246
resilience 62
ricotta
   Almond–ricotta spread 165
   Minty ricotta spread 44
rose-petal tea 191
rosehip oil 191
rosemary 191

S

sadness 66, 246
sage 191
salads
    Brekkie salad with poached eggs 47
    Broccoli 'couscous' salad 84–5
    Emmami salad 98
    Grapefruit and avo salad 92
    Kale Waldorf salad with real mayo dressing 82
    Mexicana avo salad 88
    Rainbow yoga bowl with green hummus 86–7
    Seaweed salad 90–1
    Summer slaw with blueberries and homemade mayo 81
salmon, boning 107
Salmon, kale and dill omelette 50
salt 11
Salted caramel and cinnamon macadamias 145
Seaweed salad 90–1
seeds 10
self-respect 7, 16, 243
self-talk 59, 185
Simple sauerkraut 78
skin, foods for 135
skin conditions 227
skin products 132
sleep 22, 130
slices
    Beanie brownie 160–1
    Karina's pretty raspberry and coconut slice 158
    Mango, macadamia and lemon myrtle slice 162
    Quinoa surprise slice 72
smelly feet 227
smoothies 196, 198
    Blueberry muffin smoothie 212
    Choc mousse smoothie bowl with crunchy topping 214
    Chocolate brownie smoothie 204
    Green heavy lifter 202
    Hawaiian happiness 210–11
    Smoothie toppers 200
    Turmeric anti-inflammatory smoothie 207
soup, Chunky health nerd 96
Spiced apple crumble paleo cake 174
spices 10
spirituality 178, 190, 240
spray cleaner, homemade 137
stevia 11, 18, 142
Sticky date pancakes with coconut yoghurt 36–7
stimulants 130
strength training, foods for 117
sugar 11, 22, 142
    alternatives 18, 142
    artificial sweeteners 18
    daily intake 16, 18
    effects on body 22
    reducing 16, 18
Summer slaw with blueberries and homemade mayo 81
Summer sunset 218, 219
sunshine 187
sustainable food 22
sweet potato
    Porterhouse with kale and sweet spud mash 110
    Quinoa surprise slice 72
    Rainbow yoga bowl with green hummus 86–7
    Sweet potato and pecan crumble 168
    Sweet spud and kale bites with avocado dressing 71

T

tahini 11
task lists 130
teas 11, 196, 224
    Chilled-out chamomile tea slushie 208
    see also herbal teas
therapy 56, 195, 244
thought patterns 52, 66
thyme 191
tisanes *see* herbal teas
toxins 132
travel 258
    and exercise 264
    and healthy eating 258, 262
    hydration 262
    and sleep 264
triglycerides 22
Turmeric anti-inflammatory smoothie 207

U

Unicorn cupcakes with bee pollen icing 166

V

values 64–5, 243, 256
Vanilla coconut sugar 149
vanilla pods 11
Vedic meditation 182
veggies, Moroccan nights 102–3
vulnerability 240

W

Waldorf dressing 82
water 18
    daily intake 18
    in nature 187
weight loss 22, 24, 116
    foods for 117
whole grains 117
Whole roasted cauliflower with almond butter sauce 94
work 248

Y

yoga 116, 118, 265
yoga at home 120, 130
    arm balances 128
    heart-opener poses 126–7
    hip-opener poses 127–8
    restorative poses 129
    Salute to the sun A 122–5, 265
    warm-up 120–1
yoghurt 11

Z

Zucchini and pumpkin loaf with minty ricotta spread 44–5

A Plum book

First published in 2016 by
Pan Macmillan Australia Pty Limited
Level 25, 1 Market Street,
Sydney, NSW 2000, Australia

Level 1, 15–19 Claremont Street,
South Yarra, Victoria 3141, Australia

Text copyright © Lola Berry 2016
Photographs copyright © Eve Wilson 2016, except polaroid images on pages 20, 21, 58, 63, 117, 192 and 254 © Lola Berry

The moral right of the author has been asserted.

Design and flower mandala art by Michelle Mackintosh
Paper-cut mandala art by Emma van Leest
Photography by Eve Wilson
Prop and food styling by Karina Duncan
Food preparation by Emma Christian, Kylie McAllester and Emma Warren
Edited by Miriam Cannell
Typeset by Pauline Haas
Index by Jo Rudd

Colour reproduction by Splitting Image Colour Studio
Printed and bound in China by 1010 Printing International Limited

A CIP catalogue record for this book is available from the National Library of Australia.

All rights reserved. No part of this book may be reproduced or transmitted by any person or entity (including Google, Amazon or similar organisations), in any form or means, electronic or mechanical, including photocopying, recording, scanning or by any information storage and retrieval system, without prior permission in writing from the publisher.

The publisher would like to thank the following for their generosity in providing props for the book: Arro Home, Bonnie and Neil, Home-Work and Kaz Morton Ceramics. The publisher would also like to thank Power Living Fitzroy and Parks Victoria for providing locations for the book.

David Gillespie quote on page 14 reprinted with permission from *Eat Real Food* (Pan Macmillan, 2015).

10 9 8 7 6 5 4 3 2 1